Developing a Compensation Plan for Your Library

PAULA M. SINGER

**AMERICAN
LIBRARY
ASSOCIATION**
Chicago and London
2002

Paula Singer is the principal consultant of The Singer Group, Inc., a management consulting firm she founded in 1983. Her firm provides compensation consulting, strategic planning, organization design and development, performance management, and other services to clients in the public, private, and not-for-profit sectors. Singer has been engaged as a consultant by a number of large and small library systems to custom-design compensation and salary administration plans.

Singer serves on the faculties of Johns Hopkins University and Nova Southeastern University. She is a member of the Advisory Board for the Masters of Arts in Organizational Management of the Fielding Institute and the International Advisory Board of Governors for the Center for Career Development at Maine Technical College. She has three times been honored as one of Maryland's Top 100 Women of the year. Singer holds a Ph.D. in human and organization systems. She attended Cornell and Johns Hopkins Universities and the Fielding Graduate Institute. She is married to Michael Pearlman and lives in Baltimore, Maryland.

The paper used in this publication meets the minimum requirements of American National Standard for Information Sciences—Permanence of Paper for Printed Library Materials, ANSI Z39.48-1992. ∞

Library of Congress Cataloging-in-Publication Data

Singer, Paula M.
    Developing a compensation plan for your library / Paula M. Singer.
       p.   cm.
    Includes index.
    ISBN 0-8389-0816-0 (alk. paper)
    1. Library employees—Salaries, etc.—United States.   2. Library employees—Job descriptions—United States.   3. Job evaluation—United States.   4. Job analysis.
I. Title.
Z682.3 .S53 2002
023′.9—dc21

2001056154

Printed in the United States of America.

06 05 04 03 02   5 4 3 2 1

Contents

Figures

Worksheets

Acknowledgments

I want to thank The Singer Group's library system clients, especially those in Maryland where we first began working with libraries. In particular, my gratitude goes to Linda Mielke, Muffie Smith, and Gail Griffith of Carroll County (Maryland) Public Library, Lynn Lockwood of Baltimore County Public Library, and Frieda Weiss of the University of Maryland Health System Library for their time, insights, and support.

A book is never a one-person effort. I learned a great deal about urban libraries working with Gladys Maharam and Jane Dayton of the Carnegie Library of Pittsburgh and Linda Saferite of Tulsa City–County Library. Kathleen Reif, Irene Padilla, Linda Brammer, Sharon Marshall, and Raineyl Coiro are a few of the library directors in Maryland whose experience and knowledge about county and regional libraries added value to our work together. Many examples in this book were taken from work done with the library systems they direct.

There are four others without whose contributions this book would not have been possible: my associate, Laura Hedeman, for her ideas and value added editing; Joan Grygel, my very patient, persistent, and hard-working editor; pal and writing buddy Christi Olson; and most of all my husband, Dr. Michael Pearlman, who was supportive of my writing this book even when it took time away from him and added chores to his list. Thank you all.

Introduction

Libraries that may not have the human and financial resources to commit to strategic planning or organizational development projects will fight for the resources to examine and update their compensation and pay plans. They realize that they *can't afford* not to attend to what they pay their staff, especially in a tight labor market where unemployment is low and it is difficult to recruit and retain qualified and productive employees.

Although pay is not the only factor that has an impact on the recruitment, motivation, and retention of staff, it is certainly an important one because turnover is very costly. In addition, since the library environment of today is one marked by competition and customer service, the members of your workforce can "make or break" your system's circulation and reputation. Libraries need to have pay policies that allow them to recruit and retain high-quality, motivated staff at every level and to ensure that employees are paid fairly and equitably. The challenge is to design an affordable, realistic compensation strategy that is appropriate for your culture, objectives, and strategy while being both internally equitable and competitive with the external market.

In our current economy, Wal-Mart and McDonald's are hiring entry-level staff at pay rates that exceed minimum wage and sometimes include benefits, incentives, profit sharing, or other bonus opportunities. Therefore, for some positions a library's competition for hiring qualified staff does not simply come from the public or academic library in the next county. The competition for attracting new staff and keeping current staff expands to include other employers who, although they may not be in the same "business," may offer a compensation package that influences people to change jobs or indeed careers.

PURPOSE OF THIS BOOK

A clear need exists for increased attention to compensation planning and administration in libraries. However, given the complexity and resource-intensive nature of compensation studies and structure design, how can libraries move forward in this arena without a significant infusion of budgetary resources for external consultants?

Some libraries have successfully established an internal compensation planning team rather than contracting out the complete project to consultants. The consultant's role with these teams has been to help them design a compensation process that best fits the organization, its resources, and its future. Based on personal experiences with these teams and their successes, *Developing a Compensation Plan for Your Library* was created to help libraries develop and support an internal team in the process of designing a compensation plan that

> supports the library's strategic and other long-range plans

> reflects the compensation philosophy of the library system

> is flexible and meets the needs of the library

This book is written to meet the following four goals:

1. Provide library staff with an overview of the planning steps necessary before a compensation study begins.

2. Educate the library's staff overseeing the work of consultants about the compensation process and help them maximize the benefit of this relationship, *or* provide libraries with tools to undertake the design of a compensation program if they choose to do it themselves.

3. Identify issues pertaining to compensation and link them to broader organizational and strategic issues.

4. Provide an overview of current issues in compensation and reward systems including a discussion of nonmonetary strategies and employee retention.

WHAT'S IN THIS BOOK FOR YOU?

You might be wondering, what is a compensation system? What does this have to do with me? We don't have a compensation plan—do we?

You might think you don't have a compensation system, but if you are paying employees, you do. Every library system needs to determine what employees should be paid, and each system must decide how that payment decision will be made. It must also know what it can afford to pay and how to allocate its salary budget in a way that will effectively move the system toward meeting its goals.

A compensation program is a tool—that's all. It is a business tool that should be designed to help your library meet its goals and objectives. While the cost of labor is critical to any organization, it is especially important in libraries where salaries and benefits are the largest expense.

Some say, "Money doesn't matter," especially in mission-driven organizations such as libraries and other service or nonprofit organizations. Others say, "We're in it for the public good," or "It's our contribution to society." Many say these should be the mantras of library personnel. However, library personnel do not work only for the love of the job: They need to pay bills and buy groceries too. Pay has a direct bearing on the standard of living enjoyed by most employees as well as upon the status and recognition they are able to gain. It also serves as a measure of their relative worth in comparison with other employees. If there is an objective system for determining the value of each person's job and for making each person aware of this determination, employees are less likely to perceive themselves as being victims of inequity.

In recent years it has become fashionable among some theorists to minimize the importance of pay in comparison with other motivators. While it is possible that pay does fail to motivate employees in some organizations to the extent that it should, this failure is most likely due to the way in which compensation plans are developed or administered rather than to employees' disinterest in money. The implementation of thoughtful and well-designed compensation programs can contribute effectively to meeting the objectives of your library system.

Compensation management plays a key role in human resources development within any organization. It has an impact upon all facets of human resources:

Recruitment   Rates of pay can impede or aid recruitment, and the supply of applicants can affect wage rates.

Selection   Rates of pay can affect the degree of selectivity, and selection standards affect the rate of pay required.

Training and development   The rate of pay can motivate training efforts, and training and development can lead to higher rates of pay.

Performance evaluation Performance evaluation can be a factor determining rates of pay, and wage rates can bias evaluation of performance.

Employee/labor relations Employee perceptions of unfair pay administration practices or pay rates at an extreme variance with the market may contribute to employee-relations issues or encourage employees to pursue third-party representation (unionization).

Furthermore, the importance of paying attention to creating or updating your compensation program at this time is reinforced by national trends that are placing greater importance on

- high-performance workplace initiatives
- competitive employment practices
- strategic employee retention
- time off, flextime, telecommuting, and work and family relations
- new methods for training and development

WHO SHOULD READ THIS BOOK?

Developing a Compensation Plan for Your Library is a handbook for library professionals, staff, and human resources personnel. It is also a resource for members of compensation review teams working in public, academic, and special libraries as well as in the nonprofit sector. Students learning about human resources and human resources consultants will find this book useful as well.

HOW TO USE THIS BOOK

This book will tell you how to conduct a salary survey, analyze the data, and use it to design a pay plan that fits your culture. It will lay out the steps of the process and show you how to analyze jobs, write job descriptions, and plan for communications. Figures and worksheets provide spreadsheets, letters, job descriptions, and PowerPoint presentations

that you can adapt for your use. Chapter 1 helps you think through your compensation program objectives and goals. It provides worksheets to help you get started with your compensation study. Chapter 2 focuses on the commitment you will need to obtain from the library director, board of trustees, employees, your staff association or labor union (if any), and elected or appointed officials. This chapter will help you plan your strategy for obtaining commitment from various stakeholders and provides a sample employee communications plan and examples of employee committee/task force charters. In this chapter you begin to focus on your own compensation program objectives.

In chapters 3 and 4 you will have an opportunity to learn how to obtain information about the work performed and accomplished by library system employees and how to write job descriptions using the data you collect. Job descriptions will help you identify the essential functions of each job and then use this information to assess the external value of each position.

In the fifth chapter, some of the important issues regarding the library's compensation philosophy and pay policy are mentioned for you to think through in the context of your library system. Your compensation philosophy will ultimately guide the many decisions you make as you conduct the study.

Chapter 6 lays the groundwork for deciding whether to conduct an in-depth study of the internal equity of the library's position. If you choose this route, a detailed process for designing and applying a point factor plan is provided.

Regardless of any other choices about how a hierarchical ordering of positions is made, it is strongly recommended that you learn of the wage rates offered by those in your labor market. Salary and other data can be obtained by conducting a custom survey or purchasing published salary data. Procedures for doing so, along with a sample custom survey and tools for analysis, can be found in chapter 7.

Chapter 8 focuses on designing the salary structure. With the information from the internal analysis and external market review, you can put it all together and create a salary structure that is custom-designed for your library.

Chapter 9 takes you away from "doing" to implementing and contains tips for "selling," communicating, and administering your system's new compensation plan. The salary administration section includes sections on budgeting; how to move employees through their salary ranges; best practices when facing and solving issues pertaining to salary compression; and policies for promotions, demotions, and acting-capacity pay. Finally, chapter 10 closes with trends in compensation and performance management.

This book is partly about human resources strategy, part philosophical and part "how to." It offers something for those who like to plan cautiously as well as for those who want to jump right in. You can read the chapters that focus on your need—or better yet, read those that are the *opposite* of what you are inclined to read, and broaden your perspective.

The design and implementation of compensation and pay plans are as much an art as a science. Both will be referred to in this book. Although an effort was made to distinguish between the two, sometimes the lines blur and the distinction is difficult.

The examples offered are just that—examples. What works for one library may—or may not—work for yours. Custom fit your review team and the project process to your culture, organizational structure, short- and long-term plans, and labor market. Also consider the readiness of your system to make changes as well as the budget available to support them. For example, if your library is part of a municipal or county system, or if your employees are members of a labor union or association, you may be constrained in certain areas or you may need to add additional steps or be more creative. The important thing to keep in mind is that the pay plans you develop must fit *your* library system.

1

Compensation Program Objectives

While you will have your own goals for undertaking a compensation study (which you will have the opportunity to explore in this chapter), the "bottom line" objectives of your compensation program are to support meeting the library's strategic objectives and to fit the program with its organizational structure. Compensation systems are not ends in themselves; they are a means to an end.

Compensation plans should be designed to reward employee behaviors that the library system wants to promote. For example, a library that encourages employees to return to school for a bachelor degree or an MLS will have some different pay policies and practices from an academic library that mainly recruits candidates already holding an MLS degree. Similarly, a system that wants to reward employee longevity will have a different compensation plan from a system that places a high premium on goal achievement. Finally, libraries that are planning to downsize, reorganize to use MLS positions only at the management level, or open branches in many new communities will have different goals and consequently different compensation plans.

YOUR COMPENSATION PROGRAM

While you have some specific expectations for your compensation program, you also need to make some general assumptions. For example, your program must be affordable and should

> effectively support the attraction, motivation, and retention of the number and kinds of employees you need
>
> be externally competitive
>
> gain employee acceptance
>
> be seen as equitable and fair
>
> be in compliance with federal, state, and local laws

play a positive role in motivating employees to perform to the best of their abilities

provide employees with the opportunities to achieve reasonable aspirations within the framework of impartiality and equity

provide employees with an incentive to improve their skills and abilities

be flexible enough to be revised in the future in response to changing internal and external factors

have the acceptance of the library's director and its board of trustees

be reasonable and proportionate to the resources of the library and to the priority demands of other human resource functions in terms of its nature, scope, and cost

be consistent with the library's mission, culture, and budget

While these expectations are fairly self-explanatory, the last one suggests that the compensation program cannot be "one size fits all." Even though the focus of this book is *libraries,* the compensation program that is developed must "fit" your system. That is, it should fit your

strategic and tactical plans

"business" (public, academic, or special library; central versus regional versus branch library)

demographics—both customers and employees

Regarding your strategies, you will need to think about the library's

mission What is your purpose? Why do you exist?

culture What are your beliefs, norms, values, and management style? How do employees work together?

external environment What is your labor market; pool of qualified candidates; competition with libraries, sellers of print and nonprint media, and the Internet; relationship with city/county/university; relationship with other funding sources?

legal environment What are your union agreements, human resources policies, and related legislation and legal mandates?

COMPENSATION AND THE HUMAN RESOURCES SYSTEM

Compensation is one component of your human resources system, which also includes recruitment, performance management systems, training and development, employee relations, and so forth. Each of these facets of human resources management/ development has an impact on the others and together they make up the whole. The same is true of compensation. In addition to having a compensation plan, your library's compensation plan is part of a total compensation *system,* which includes the benefits received by employees, both direct (pay) and indirect (benefits) compensation. Examples of what is included in both of these categories are shown in figure 1.1.

TOTAL COMPENSATION

The components of a pay system, however, go beyond the two major categories of direct and indirect compensation, or, simply, the financial aspects. That is, total compensation includes a *total rewards* strategy:

compensation wages and bonuses

benefits paid time off and insurance

social interaction friendly workplace

status/recognition respect and prominence due to work

task variety opportunities to experience different things

workload right amount of work

work importance society's value of work

authority/control/autonomy ability to influence others and control destiny

advancement opportunities to get ahead

feedback constructive help for development

work conditions hazard-free workplaces

FIGURE 1.1 Components of Direct and Indirect Compensation

Direct Compensation

Base pay
Differential pay
  • evenings, weekends, holidays
Short- and long-term incentive pay
Pay for performance
Cash recognition and achievement awards

Indirect Compensation

Legally required benefits
  • worker's compensation
  • social security
  • unemployment insurance
Other benefits
  • Health insurance
  • Short- and long-term disability insurance
  • Deferred pay
  • Pension
  • Paid time off
      holidays and sick, vacation, and personal leave
  • Tuition reimbursement
  • Unpaid leave
  • Noncash recognition and achievement awards
  • Perquisites, including free parking

development opportunities formal and informal training to learn new knowledge/skills/abilities[1]

The focus of this book is primarily on *direct* compensation: how employees are paid in relation to each other and in relation to the market. However, consideration of a total rewards strategy is consistent with some of the new trends in compensation in both the private and public sectors. (Trends, alternative compensation strategies, recruitment and retention strategies, and some of the ideas on total compensation are in chapter 10.) These trends include

moving from a culture that values internal equity to one that focuses upon performance (individual or team) and paying in accordance with the relevant market

organizationally shifting from bureaucratic, hierarchical, "command and control" structures to those that value empowerment, reduced management layers, and a broadening of job scope

Many libraries are seeing a need for reward systems that support these trends. Some libraries are not yet ready to implement new pay programs such as incentives or pay for performance because the "change is too big," "there are too many changes right now," "the board of trustees will not accept it," or "employees won't accept it." Even if you agree with those reasons, keep an open mind and think of some of these new ways of conceiving compensation as something you might want to plan for in the future.

YOUR REASONS FOR UNDERTAKING A COMPENSATION STUDY

Since you are reading this book, you are probably contemplating updating your pay plan and conducting a compensation study for one or more of a variety of reasons. The reasons that are often mentioned by libraries for undertaking this process are to

pay employees the "going" rate

decrease turnover

improve morale

control labor costs

be fair and equitable

learn of the pay and other practices of competitor organizations

position the library system to attract and retain the best and most qualified employees

reward employees for long service

reward employees for doing a great job

provide a career ladder

be able to "pirate" outstanding employees from other libraries and competitor organizations

keep up with increases in the cost of living

obtain valid data that will be helpful in labor negotiations in a union environment

seek a fair pay plan to discourage union
organization

As you can see, there are as many reasons for
conducting a study as there are types of libraries.
Some of these reasons may be yours as well, or you
might have totally different ones. Seeing a broad
set of possibilities might even spark additional
reasons for you to go ahead with the process.

Some of the unanticipated outcomes of putting
in a new compensation program have resulted in a
number of benefits to the library system. For example, the process of developing a compensation
program may improve communications between
employees and their supervisors. It also creates a
framework and tools for managers and supervisors
to use when making decisions about hiring rates
and about salary increases for promotions and transfers. A compensation system may provide justification to funding sources for budget increases.
Furthermore, it can promote flexibility when assigning employees with certain knowledge, skills, and
abilities to the new structure, thus resulting in an
effective use of the workforce for the library and
in greater career growth, development, and cross-
training for library employees.

GETTING STARTED

Now, with insight into compensation and its role in
the library system, it's time to get started. The following sections ask you to think about your goals
for undertaking the process and the motivators and
potential ramifications in engaging in a compensation study at this time. You should also reflect on
the library's strategic initiatives and how a new or
revised compensation program can support their
fulfillment.

Goals

As you contemplate what others have said about
their reasons for conducting a pay study, think
about what is motivating your library to undertake
a compensation study at this time. Following are

some compensation program goals from an academic library:

1. a market plan designed for our needs
2. a competitive pay for performance plan that
   recognizes developmental achievements,
   performance levels, and positions within a
   range
3. librarian salaries matched to faculty salaries
4. wide and deep ranges allowing for growth
   without having to achieve a higher pay level

What are *your* goals? It is important to know
what you hope to achieve and to gain consensus
about it. Every library will have different goals and
desired outcomes based upon needs, strategic initiatives, labor market, budget, culture, and human
resource philosophy. Furthermore, while the study
will have to take place within parameters, it will be
conducted within the context of your environment.
That is, your goals may be enhanced or limited if
you are required to adhere to certain local government or university policies. Goals, therefore, should
be unique to your library and established within
any parameters that exist. *Do not, however, limit
your creativity based on funding or other perceived
barriers.* Set goals and design the compensation
plan to fit your library. Scaling back, or phasing
implementation if necessary, can come later. Use
worksheet 1 to write a list of your goals for a successful compensation study.

It is important to keep these goals in mind as
you design and implement the study. It is very easy
to get sidetracked and say, "Oh, let's look at that
too." If you know what your goals are, you will be
able to keep your priorities in order and focus on
them. Later, you will be able to evaluate the degree
to which your goals were met and plan for changes
in the future.

Potential Ramifications

In addition to the positive outcomes, you will want
to be aware of the potential ramifications as well.
That is, while there will be many positive outcomes
resulting from the compensation study, you should
also be aware of potential negative outcomes. This

Goals for Your Compensation Study

1. _____

2. _____

3. _____

4. _____

5. _____

is not mentioned to deter you from undertaking a study but to raise your awareness and alert you to the possibility of problems. If alerted, you will be able to plan ahead to avoid or minimize the impact of negative outcomes. Some actual experiences of libraries follow:

Staff learned that their pay rates were below the market.

Management and employees learned that their pay rates were *above* the market rate—and read about it in the newspaper, thus causing morale problems.

The board of trustees did not approve the compensation plan.

Funds to implement the plan were not obtained.

The hierarchical ordering of positions was not reflective of the current or proposed organizational structure and realities of work.

Streamlined jobs led to the ability to eliminate positions or to combine some into lower graded jobs.

Morale issues developed with employees assigned a job title in a perceived lower grade level.

Employees yearned to maintain the status quo and resisted updated, flexible job descriptions.

Employees who did not receive expected salary increases had decreased morale.

Are these scenarios really possible? Yes. All have indeed happened—luckily not all to the same client. You will need to be prepared for these possibilities, just in case. Some of these "negatives," however, turned out to be positive. Employees and managers just did not perceive them that way at the time.

You should also be aware of the possible unanticipated negative outcomes that might emerge during or as a result of your project. Think about what they might be and how they can be minimized. Worksheet 2 provides two examples of a plan to combat possible negative ramifications. Complete the worksheet with your own possibilities. As you read the rest of this book you will gain insights into ways to combat potential negatives. Use the second column to briefly jot down your ideas while reading the rest of this book.

Focusing on Your Library

Your library is unlike any other library. Having reviewed your goals for conducting a compensation study, it's time to reflect upon who you are. Doing so will help identify some of your human resource planning needs as you head into the future. Once you have a clearer picture or have reviewed where you are and are aware of your needs for competent staff, you will be able to clarify your library's compensation needs.

Plan to Combat Possible Negative Ramifications

Possible Negative Results	Minimize by
(Example) Employees are frustrated, as we do not have the funds to implement recommendations.	Budget for, or ascertain where funds might be available for the possible fiscal impact to implement; create a 1–3-year implementation plan.
(Example) Employees don't accept the changes.	Involve employees as much as possible; seek their input via questionnaires, interviews, and focus groups; create a cross-functional review committee; communicate; set realistic goals and expectations.
1.	
2.	
3.	
4.	

Define your library system by answering the questions on worksheet 3. Your answers to these questions will tell you more about your library and your strategic objectives. If you've recently engaged in a planning process, undoubtedly you will have already answered these and many other questions.[2]

If yours is like many libraries, two things will be quickly evident from worksheet 3: First, unless you recently went through a planning process, you may not know the answers to many of these questions. Second, the library is probably already undergoing some type of change process or considering major changes.

A Changing Environment Most organizations are not static; this is particularly true of libraries in recent years. The technology has changed tremendously in a very short period of time and will continue to do so at an even more rapid pace. This is evident in changes needed in employee skill levels, which vary greatly: On one hand you might see sixteen-year-old pages in suburban branches designing Web pages and teaching Internet search skills. On the other, you might see librarians who graduated from library school many years ago and circulation assistants who think that if they wait long enough, the computers will go away—or they will wait it out until they retire. Should these librarians be paid alike? Indeed, what type of work should they be doing?

Budget Issues Many library systems are facing budget issues. Some are in crisis, and others are obtaining increasing support from their educational institutions, local governments, philanthropic and fundraising efforts, or foundations.

Competition for Employees The competition for recent MLS graduates is increasing. Many new graduates decide to cash in on their information management skills in corporate America where

Your Library Definition

1. What is the role of your library?

   What is your mission? Why does your library system exist?

2. What do you do?

   Do you have a strong children's program and often need to recruit children's librarians? Is outreach or technology crucial?

3. What is your organization structure?

   Do you have a flat structure with few levels? Do employees work in teams? Is individual contribution highly valued?

4. Who is your competition?

   Is your competition limited to other local libraries, or must you be aware of what other nonprofit organizations are paying? What about academic institutions? The private sector? Local government? Do you compete with the local school board for librarians and media specialists?

5. What is your financial situation?

   Do you have the funds to implement even small adjustments if employee salaries fall below a minimum market rate? Can you afford not to? Can you afford to pay above market rates to recruit and retain the highest performers?

6. What are your other relationships?

   With your community? With funding sources/political entities if you are a public library? With the university if you are an academic library? If you need additional funds for implementation, will you have support from the community, local government, foundations, or university? Does this community perceive your service as critical? Is it perceived as high quality?

7. What are your goals and objectives?

   For the next year? For your three-to-five-year strategic plan? Do the members of the library's staff have the skills to meet these objectives? If so, will they be rewarded for having them? If not, will you hire employees who have these skills? Will you train incumbents?

8. How do your board and senior management view human resources?

   Are employees perceived as costs or investments? Are they to be cultivated or do you expect a high turnover? Are employees viewed as just another expense item or as human capital?

the opportunity to earn more money is greater, instead of applying for positions in public or academic libraries.

Role of Your Library In this time of dynamic change, the role of library personnel in today's academic and public libraries is being examined. To what tasks and responsibilities should an MLS employee be assigned? Can an employee with a BA in music and some training provide similar services to customers? What is a customer anyway? Didn't they used to be called patrons? Libraries around the country are looking at their roles for the first time. Should they be like Barnes and Noble? Why? Should they adopt the Wal-Mart model of customer service? The Nordstrom model?

These are important issues to think about as you design a compensation program. They determine the type of jobs that you need, the duties assigned to each, and the minimum amount of experience and education required of each incumbent.

If you believe that your system will be changing in the next few years, it is best to design a system that is flexible and responsive to frequent changes. Throughout this book, examples of both traditional and more flexible models of compensation management and salary administration are given.

Notes

1. G. T. Mikovich and J. M. Newman, *Compensation,* 5th ed. (Homewood, Ill.: Irwin, 1996), 18.
2. See, for example, Sandra Nelson for the Public Library Assn., *The New Planning for Results: A Streamlined Approach* (Chicago: American Library Assn., 2001).

2

Preliminary Planning

This chapter discusses the steps to consider before embarking on a compensation study: obtaining commitment, developing communications, and considering the pros and cons of using consultants and of chartering a committee. Also included is a sample letter and a PowerPoint presentation that could be adapted for preproject communications to employees.

COMMITMENT AND INVOLVEMENT

Obtaining commitment before the project begins is critical. You should not begin a project like this without obtaining the commitment of your library director, board of trustees, any union or staff association that may be involved, the city/county/university if your library is a department within one of these larger entities, and library employees. These stakeholders have a voice or a perspective that is important to consider and include in any project planning.

Time

People are often surprised at the amount of time and effort that is required of the project manager and human resources staff. They are less surprised by the costs of engaging consultants to conduct the study than they are by the amount of their own time and effort that is required throughout the project, whether consultants are enlisted or not.

Money

In addition, the team conducting the study is likely to recommend changes that cost money and change the status quo. Do *not* undertake a major review of your compensation or classification plans unless you have the budgeted funds or can obtain the resources to fund the recommendations of the study at least partially. Also, do not commit to an implementation plan if it cannot be at least partially funded in the first year.

There are several reasons for this: It is not fair to psychologically "set up" employees for change if there is no budget for implementation. While it is important to clarify expectations with employees at the outset of the project (i.e., they should not expect raises), most have the expectation of fair treatment assuming that changes in salary grade or compensation will be attempted and recommendations budgeted into the fiscal planning process. If this does not happen, morale will be adversely affected.

Feedback

Projects that do not include follow-up or feedback to employees following a study are likely to result in negative feelings toward administration. In these circumstances, when the library system is ready to go ahead, employees may understandably be apathetic. Some employees may remark "Oh yeah, another compensation study. . . . Nothing happened with the last one, so nothing will happen with this one either." It then takes time to rebuild trust and enthusiasm for employee involvement. Understand that involvement leads to buy-in, and buy-in is necessary for acceptance, support, and implementation. Therefore, it is important to be clear about the anticipated outcomes at the outset.

Stakeholders

Buy-in and commitment from several stakeholders are critical to the success of this project. In addition to employees, the key stakeholders are the library director, board of trustees, and staff association or union. If the library is a department or unit of a city, county, or university, the human resources department or even the city manager might be a key stakeholder as well. While some of these stakeholders, the library director and board of trustees in particular, are key decision makers and the others may not be, it is still important to gain all stake-

holders' commitment to the project or, at the very least, inform them about it.

The Library Director

The director of the library needs to support the project because he or she needs to commit the resources in terms of both staff time and funds. The library director should also approve the project's process including the use and selection of a project manager, review committee, or consultants. The director should shape the compensation philosophy, which will ultimately guide the design of a new compensation plan. With staff help, the library director must also "make the case" to go ahead with such a project to the library's board of directors or trustees.

The Board

Often, a project budget is developed and funds set aside with the concurrence of the board. Budgets are a concern at this preplanning stage if consultants are to be retained to support the project or if other resources are needed. The library's board is also usually involved if a budget allocation is necessary to fund implementation. That is, if findings indicate that salary adjustments are warranted to maintain internal or external equity, it is important to ensure that the budget funds are available. Many boards of trustees are interested in potential salary inequities and want to correct them if they exist. They also want to make sure that employees are fairly compensated and that salary ranges are designed to recruit and retain qualified staff.

The board should be included as important stakeholders in the preliminary planning and "go/no go" decision phase of the compensation study and should receive planned periodic updates that will minimize end-of-project surprises when findings or recommendations are presented. There is no one best way to involve the board of directors. Each library system board is different and has different ways of working. It is important to respect these differences and communicate with members in the most appropriate way. Educating trustees about the compensation study is helpful in gaining that commitment. Education and involvement early in the process enhance approval and acceptance of the study.

You can work with boards of trustees in a variety of ways. For example, in a study for a small library system, a member of the board of trustees participated as a member of the compensation committee. While he didn't attend every meeting, he was informed about the process. In this case, both the executive director and assistant director also served on the committee. This is more common in smaller library systems, where there is a very small or no human resources staff. A side benefit of this level of involvement was that the board member became more connected with the library and its staff. Staff also became more appreciative of the board and its role in library governance.

Another example comes from a medium-sized public library system that serves the library needs of both urban dwellers and suburbanites. During the course of this project the consultant met with and gave periodic reports to the board of trustees' human resources committee. When the time came to present findings to the library's board of trustees, the human resources committee members made an unequivocal endorsement because of their understanding of the system and process. This vote of confidence in the findings and recommendations helped to pave the way to approval and funding.

Another way of connecting with board members occurred with a medium-sized public library in a suburban community of Baltimore. In this situation, the four to five members of the board's human resources committee, the library's deputy director, and the human resources director and assistant composed the steering committee.

Staff Association or Union

Involve the staff association or union as well if you have one. Sometimes compensation studies are conducted as a result of a negotiation or "meet and confer" process, where both the union and management agree to collect valid salary data to determine pay rates. If your library system has a collective bargaining agreement or memorandum of understanding with a union or labor association, review it before taking action to ensure that no violations

will occur. Some agreements or memorandums provide for the involvement of the labor union or association in a variety of ways including the selection of consultants (if any), the design of the study process, participation in a compensation review committee that is created, and review of findings and recommendations before they are presented to the library board for approval. If you are a party to any such agreement, follow the stipulated process.

Even if there is no agreement for the participation of a labor union or staff association, it is a good practice to involve them. Once the library director and human resources staff have an idea of the direction in which they want to go, inform the president of the union or association and discuss his or her role. It is worthwhile and expedient to invite a union representative to serve on any committee that is created, keeping them informed and updated. The union or association should be treated like any other stakeholder group in this process. At a minimum, they should become informed, and their opinions should be sought in the data-collection process by inviting them to be interviewed and to participate as a member of a focus group.

At a large urban library, the president of the staff association, a branch manager, was viewed as an important stakeholder. She was interviewed early in the process for the staff association's perspective on compensation and classification issues, problems, and needs and served as a member of the review committee and job-evaluation team. In a school system, members of the negotiations team served on the review committee, and findings were presented to the entire team.

City, County, or University

Many library systems receive their funding from a city, county, or university. Some libraries have their own personnel and compensation processes and policies that are separate and distinct from these funding sources, while others are a part of the larger administrative structure.

If the library requires additional funds to minimize inequities, you may need to go to the city or county administrator or council or the university for support. Therefore, it is important to schedule a discussion with the human resources or finance director even before you get started in the process for several reasons. First, they might be able to provide you with resources such as their human resources staff, salary data, experience performing similar studies, best practices, and so forth. Second, they will let you know if there are reasons why you should not undertake a study at this time. For example, there may be no extra funding available if it is needed for implementation, or there might be plans to conduct a similar study and they may invite your participation. You should ascertain whether you have the flexibility to design your own system or to identify the parameters you must follow as part of the larger compensation system.

Some library systems are a department of a local government. In these cases, the library is usually not given the "go-ahead" to conduct an independent study of its classifications. However, exceptions have been made when recruitment or retention problems arise due to insufficient salaries. The same holds true with colleges and universities.

In a recent campuswide study for a large East coast university, the director of the professional library served as a member of the advisory committee. Because of her involvement, the study addressed library issues. Since this was a market-based study, extra efforts were made to designate as many library positions as possible as benchmark (surveyed) positions. (See chapter 7.) Therefore, salary information was collected for those positions. Issues of faculty appointments for librarians were addressed as an outcome of the study, as were concerns pertaining to the technology skills required.

Where the library system is a department (as opposed to an agency) of local government, it is most likely that library positions will be studied when all positions are reviewed as part of an organizationwide compensation study. When the library department is a separate agency, the choice is more likely to be the library's. Whenever the library system has the option it should do its *own* study. The reasons relate to time, attention, and focus. If you are doing your own study, your consultants or your staff review committee are totally focused on library, and only library, positions. In this scenario,

all library positions and issues can be studied. This is not the case when the library's positions are studied along with those in the departments of public works, planning and zoning, and social services in local government or, in a university system, along with student services, financial aid, academic affairs, and finance and administration.

Having said this, one way to enhance your position in a large-scale or organizationwide study is to *be involved.* Don't wait for the university or local government human resources director to come to you. As soon as you learn that a compensation study is being considered, *"run, don't walk"* to volunteer to participate in the process. If consultants will be retained, offer your services as a member of the selection or evaluation team. Ask the top three consultants who submitted proposals if they have experience with library systems. Once the project begins, ask to be included on the list of stakeholders to be interviewed, and ask to be made a member of the compensation steering or review committee. Yes, it will take precious time that you and your staff do not have; however, it will be more than worth it as your presence enables you to bring your library system's issues to the table. An extra benefit to this level of participation for your library system is that you will learn a great deal and find yourself educated about the compensation systems and processes that govern the library.

Employees

The same philosophy of involvement holds true for employees. Frankly, no project will be completely successful without this involvement. Build employee commitment by creating a communications plan that educates and later updates them about the project, talk to them and ask for their input, and ask them about their jobs.

Complete worksheet 4 to help plan your strategy for obtaining commitment and a "go ahead" for the library's compensation study. Taking the time to go through this worksheet will help you assess who your stakeholders are in this compensation study and the level of involvement you need them to have.

Plan to Engage Stakeholders

Stakeholder	Gain Commitment	Provide Information	Date and by Whom	Possible Issues and Expected Outcomes
Library director	Importance of project Process Who will be involved Time and financial commitment	Presentation or conversation		
Library trustees/ board of directors	Importance of project Financial commitment Process	Presentation about process Input about compensation philosophy		
Labor union/ staff association	Process Role	Interviews Participation as committee member		
City/county/university finance director, human resources director	Relationship of compensation systems Funding issues	Human resources interviews Human resources participation on committee		
Employees	Process Role Expectations	Focus groups Interviews Project updates Representation on review committee		

Although some information has been filled in for you, delete or add to this plan as appropriate for your library's needs and organization.

In column 1, determine which stakeholders need to be informed about the compensation study. Next, plan what you need to tell or ask the members of each of these stakeholder groups. In the third column include some considerations in working with each of these groups. For example, when informing the board about the compensation project, you might give a presentation about the process and ask for its input in defining the library's compensation philosophy. Complete the date this will be done and by whom. Finally, note issues that might arise or outcomes you can expect from gaining commitment from each of these stakeholders.

COMMUNICATIONS

The communications plan should continue throughout the process of the compensation study. Members of the review team should be held accountable for providing updates to stakeholders on a regular basis. As with gaining the commitment of all stakeholders, it is also important to keep each group informed about the project through its life. Continual and regular communication is the key. Figure 2.1 shows the outline for a communications plan with the various stakeholders. Of course, the board and employees are critical stakeholders in this process. Therefore, the following sections specifically address communications with these two groups.

Board Communications

Depending upon the nature and structure of the board, sometimes consultants meet with board members or the executive or human resources committee early in the project to present a communications session and ask for their input, expectations, and ideas. Consideration should be given to discussing compensation philosophy with trustees as

FIGURE 2.1 Sample Communications Plan

Purpose	To Whom	What	By Whom	How	Date
Introduce study	All stakeholders	Outline steps Manage expectations Introduce team and/or consultants List questions and answers	Library director or project manager	Interlibrary mail Intranet Face-to-face group meetings Videoconference	Week 1
Feedback	Employees	Findings from interviews or focus groups	Project manager	Intranet Letter Meetings	Weeks 4–5
Updates	Employees, managers, board, staff association or union	Findings and project status	Project manager or team member	Intranet E-mail newsletter	Ongoing following team/staff meetings or monthly
Findings and recommendations	Board and, upon board approval, all stakeholders	Summary of findings and recommendations Changes and impact on employees	Project manager, committee members, or consultants	Letter Newsletter Individualized letter Frequently asked questions	At the end of the project after board approval

well because this may result in a changed policy direction.

Without ongoing updates, board members who are uninformed may say, "Why didn't you consider *X* Library when collecting data?" or, "I think we should pay our employees above the market to attract the best staff, why are you setting midpoints just at the market?" or, "We can't afford to do anything this year. We're building a new branch, ordering self-check machines. . . . Why are you doing this anyway?" Early education pays off and helps ensure a smooth approval process when findings are presented to the board.

If board members are not part of the project team, they *must* be kept informed of the various stages. For example, working with a large, East-coast library, while the consultant never met with the library's board of trustees or any of its members, she prepared presentations for the library director to give to the board. In general, at a minimum, consultants and committee members are often asked to make a final presentation to the board of the findings, recommendations, and proposed pay and classification plan. Your project manager and committee should plan to do the same.

Employee Communications

To begin the communication process with employees, an introductory letter or presentation by the project manager or library director is the first step. The letter usually states the what, why, who, when, and how of the compensation study. That is, it should clearly tell employees that the library system is about to undertake a compensation and classification study and why. If presentations are made, the library director should open the meetings, introduce the team, and generally show his or her support and leadership. The presentation or letter should provide the following information:

- the name of the project manager
- an outline of the steps involved in the project
- the names of the members of the review or steering committee and a description of their role
- the role of employees

- time frames of the project
- what employees could expect—as well as what they should not expect

Worksheet 5 is a sample form letter to employees. You may want to adapt it for your own situation.

Managing employee expectations is very important from the outset. Educating your employees about what to expect will help minimize concerns. Emphasizing the following two very important points may help alleviate some of the anxiety that often accompanies compensation studies:

- No employee will lose a job as a result of the compensation study.
- No employee will have his or her salary decreased as a result of the study.

However, employees should know that they may be asked to do their job *differently* or even to do a different job as a result of the study.

ENGAGE CONSULTANTS— OR NOT?

Early on you will have to decide whether to use consultants. Consider both the pros and cons of using consultants for your project. Your decision will also be based upon the circumstances and culture in your library system. Some of the pros and cons of using external consultants are shown in figure 2.2.

If you choose to outsource the project, find a consultant who is willing to be your partner in the process. Make it a joint effort in which the consultant brings the compensation design and implementation expertise and you—and your employees—provide the library system know-how and internal perspective of processes.

Retain a consultant who will provide ongoing education during the project so there can be a transfer of learning. Your consultant should support your goals, learning, and independence. Whomever you choose should be willing to work collaboratively with you and should be someone with whom you feel comfortable and whom you can trust. He or she should be an authentic partner in the process.

Form Letter to All Employees

Dear *<library system>* staff member:

As you know, we plan to review our compensation practices before the end of this year. To help us achieve our objectives, we have engaged an outside consultant to perform a comprehensive study of our compensation, classification, and staffing plans.

We have chosen *<insert consultants' names or name of firm>*, a management consulting firm located in *<place>*, to assist us with this project. They have extensive experience conducting these types of studies for numerous library systems, governments, nonprofit organizations, and private-sector companies.

We will have an official project kick-off meeting on *<date>*. *<Consultants' names>* will be with us for two days as we begin to define the initial steps of the project.

Briefly, this project will involve an in-depth look at our library's compensation plans and job titles both from an internal and external perspective. That is, *<consultants' names>* will work with an internal committee to analyze how our library's salaries compare to the external marketplace in addition to how our jobs compare to each other internally.

They will be asking each of you to fill out questionnaires describing your job duties and requirements and will conduct surveys of other libraries and organizations to gather external market salary data.

On *<dates>*, *<consultants' names>* will be facilitating the first compensation review committee meetings with a cross-section of library staff. This committee will serve throughout the project as a source of input and sounding board for project findings and recommendations. They will also be asked to communicate to all staff members what is happening during key phases of the project.

Compensation review committee members are:
<list committee members by name, title, and department or branch>

<Consultants' names> will also be interviewing various managers and supervisors, and they will hold six focus groups with employees at all levels to gather data about compensation, job titles, and staffing issues and concerns.

This project is a critical one to our library as it involves reviewing our compensation and staffing programs. However, it is important that you know that no employee will lose his or her job or have a salary decrease as a result of this study. On the other hand, no employee should expect a pay increase either.

The objectives of this project are to ensure that

> our salaries are in line with our identified marketplace
>
> positions are internally equitable
>
> we are staffed in a manner that is efficient and effective while providing excellent customer service

If you have any questions, please feel free to contact *<name>*, who is the project manager. She can be reached at *<telephone number and e-mail address>*.

Sincerely,

Director

FIGURE 2.2   Pros and Cons of Using External Consultants

Pros	Cons
Tend to be perceived by employees as more objective than internal employees or management	Need to learn your system, processes, people, culture, and norms
Have past experience with compensation within libraries and other organizations	May be seen as outsiders
Expertise/knowledge of what works well and what doesn't	May be costly
Credibility in designing and implementing compensation systems	May not have as much commitment to the process as would an internal team
No preconceived "agenda"	Not as invested in your library
Saves staff time to focus on day-to-day operations and customers	Still need a committee

Needless to say, the consultant should have experience working with libraries and be able to provide references.

If you choose to work with consultants, this book is still an invaluable resource. You will also want to use other resources that might be available. For example, the human resources director of your local government or college may have salary data or a process that could be helpful. Look for other books on compensation. Call your state or regional library association. Network with your colleagues who have recently completed studies.

Whether or not you retain consultants, one of the most important tasks will be to appoint a knowledgeable internal project manager with good group-facilitation and project-management skills. Second, appoint a staff member (perhaps a reference librarian) as a researcher to learn about program designs and data collection tools, and so forth.

COMMITTEE APPROACH— OR NOT?

Should there be a committee? Definitely, yes! Some colleagues don't agree, but experience has shown that the resulting buy-in is greater and learning is promoted when a committee approach is used.

Does it take longer? Yes. Couldn't the consultants do it faster and easier? Again, yes. So why

bother? Experiences gained over the years indicate that, except in very small library systems, employee acceptance and buy-in is never as good when working directly with the human resources director or library director as it is when a committee is appointed. Without a committee the number of appeals or requests for a review of the grade to which a position is slotted may be greater. In one instance a staff member went to the newspaper and a member of the board of trustees and alleged unfairness regarding study results. On a more positive note, *why not* take advantage of the opportunity for members of the library staff to

learn about compensation and classification

experience working as a member of a cross-functional team

learn more about the library system

meet fellow library employees and see them in a different light

have a chance to showcase individuals' abilities

Two stories of positive/favorable outcomes come to mind, both relating to committees. A committee was asked to do some preproject work researching issues. At the beginning of the meeting after asking for a volunteer to report findings, there was silence. A senior circulation clerk finally spoke and gave a wonderful presentation of her research. Needless to say, the ice was broken. More importantly, throughout the process this individual continued to show initiative, creativity, and ability. She was soon promoted to circulation supervisor in a mid-sized branch.

Another story—one with both good and bad outcomes for the library—involves a self-taught computer technician in a small public library. While serving on the committee, she increased her knowledge of technology, the skills that were in demand in the marketplace, and the salaries paid to information technology professionals. At the final committee meeting, she announced that she had asked the director for and had been granted a leave of absence to return to college to pursue a degree in information technology. She has since returned part-time, with more skills to offer—and a higher salary.

Committee Type

Many libraries use a design, steering, advisory, or review committee in the process of conducting a compensation study. The differences are more than a matter of semantics. Each type of committee calls for a different level of hands-on involvement and of approval and decision-making authority. In addition, different public libraries and universities convene some of these types of committees more commonly than others. Experience has taught that it is best to use the name "design committee" only when consultants are not used or where the members of the team will actually be designing and developing the new compensation philosophy, classification plan, and pay structure. In addition, use "steering committee" only when the members have decision-making authority. Advisory committees are most often used in university settings or when the members are not necessarily a cross-section of staff or are board members of the library. When working with an advisory committee, seek information from the members at the beginning of the project, including information about their perspectives on compensation issues, difficulties with recruitment and retention, compensation philosophy, and so forth. The advisory committee may not meet again until near the project's completion. During this late-term meeting ask the advisory committee to look for what might have been missed, what might not make sense in this particular system, or other mine-fields that need to be avoided.

It is best to use the term that is normally assigned by the library for employee committees. Where that is not clear, use the term "review committee." Members of a review committee generally review all findings, suggest options, discuss alternatives, and become more involved in the process as a whole than do their counterparts on advisory committees. For the remainder of this book, the committee assigned to the project is referred to as the review committee.

Committee Charter

The committee or team can be called whatever makes sense in your environment, as long as its role is *clearly defined.* That is critical. Whether or not you work with consultants, a charter should be drafted so that the expectations and purpose of the committee are clear at the outset. Figures 2.3 and 2.4 are examples of charters that you may modify and adopt for your own library system.

The advisory committee charter (figure 2.3) was taken from a slide shown at the first meeting with a large public university with which the author had contracted to design and implement a new exempt compensation program. Most of the members of this committee were department heads—assistant and

FIGURE 2.3   Compensation Committee Charter for a Public University

Advisory Committee Role
   Identify current issues
      • compensation
      • classification
      • salary administration
   Contribute ideas and feedback
      • sounding board
      • "heads up"
      • What do you think? Did we miss anything?
   React and advise
   Attend four meetings, including today

FIGURE 2.4   Compensation Committee Charter for an Urban Public Library

Compensation Review Committee

CHARGE

The compensation review committee is composed of a cross-section of library staff. The members of this committee provide input to the consultants over the life of this project. The review committee is not a steering committee nor is it the only or final group providing input to and review of this study. It is created because the consultants and library management value the input of library personnel into compensation issues.

Meetings with the review committee will be scheduled approximately every three weeks. It is currently understood and anticipated that the role of the review committee includes the following:

1. to provide input into and understanding about compensation issues currently facing the library

2. to serve as a communication link with members of the library staff

3. to provide input into or review the

    work plan

    participants' survey

    position description questionnaire

    list of benchmark positions

    miniposition descriptions

    findings

    recommendations

It is expected that members of the review committee will keep committee discussions and preliminary findings of the consultants confidential until the appropriate time.

associate vice presidents. The second charge (figure 2.4) was one given to the members of a review committee representing a cross-section of the staff of an urban library.

The important thing to keep in mind when preparing a charter is that it should state the objectives of the committee. It should also establish boundaries on what the committee will and will not review and the extent to which it serves as a review, recommending, or decision-making body. The charter might also specify the frequency of meetings, who will facilitate them, and the role the facilitator will take during meetings. Some charters outline norms or ground rules for working together. Some include all the commtitee roles, such as time-keeper, notetaker, and process observer. Keep the charter simple and consistent with other committee charters in your library.

3
Job Analysis

Before you make decisions about your compensation program, make sure you have an understanding of the work that is performed by the employees in your library system. Job analysis will provide this information.

Libraries are transformed so frequently that the tasks of yesterday may not be those needed tomorrow. A compensation study often uncovers activities that maintain the status quo—instead of those activities that promote the library's goals and plans. To enhance the library's flexibility as well as promote employee growth and development, we recommend the following:

1. Look at how work is accomplished—not just individual tasks, but how and by whom (position, not individuals) it is being done.
2. Review the library's strategic goals to ensure that the work that needs to be done to fulfill them is being done and is placed at the proper level.
3. Ensure that all work is being done at the lowest possible level.

It is generally suggested that you begin your compensation study with a complete and thorough analysis of all library jobs. Conducting this phase of work will allow you to

identify the essential job functions for each position

prepare up-to-date job descriptions reflective of your library system's culture, technology, organizational design, demographics, and skills and competencies

market price positions (good matching requires baseline information about a job's essential functions, level of responsibility, and qualifications)

comply with federal and state legislation

If you select a point factor method of job evaluation (see chapter 7) to determine your internal job hierarchy, it is particularly important to conduct the job analysis early in the process, so you have all the data you need when you begin to evaluate jobs.

This chapter defines job analysis, discusses data to collect and collection procedures, and gives a brief synopsis of legal compliance issues. Included is a sample job analysis questionnaire.

DEFINITION

Job analysis is the systematic process of collecting relevant, work-related information as to the nature, scope, and responsibilities of your library's jobs. As a result of job analysis, you will gain an understanding of and be able to document the knowledge, skills, abilities, and other factors required for each library position. Job analysis is the foundation upon which job descriptions are written and jobs are priced in the market. It is also the tool that will enable you to understand the essential functions of each position to ensure compliance with the Americans with Disabilities Act.

USES

Job analysis findings ultimately have several uses, among them proper classification of positions and current information to be used in the development of job descriptions. They can and should be used for a variety of purposes supporting human resources and strategic planning, including

designing jobs

making recruitment, selection, and placement decisions

setting performance criteria and appraisal

establishing training, job development, and career counseling programs

designing job families and career paths

ensuring compliance with legal requirements on exempt versus nonexempt status (Fair Labor Standards Act) and overtime eligibility

planning human resources

making outsourcing decisions

determining organization design

analyzing staffing patterns

analyzing work flow

Before commencing job analysis, your first step is to consider

- what information should be collected
- how the information will be collected
- who should be involved

DATA TO COLLECT

In job analysis, you will want to gather information regarding the knowledge, skills, abilities, and other factors pertaining to or required by the job. Some of the other pertinent factors include working conditions, especially if they are adverse and involve difficulty (such as excessive or extensive lifting), supervisory responsibility, or key success factors such as the ability to work as a team member. The amount of data to be collected depends on the purpose of the job analysis process, including whether the findings will be used to determine the internal equity of the library system by applying a point factor system to all jobs. (This application of job analysis to a point factor system is discussed in chapter 7.)

HOW TO COLLECT
THE INFORMATION

There are a variety of ways to collect information about jobs: observations, interviews, job analysis questionnaires (JAQs), or work diaries or logs. Figure 3.1 lists the methods used to collect information about the positions in your library system. A description of each method includes the types of jobs for which each method is most appropriate and the advantages and disadvantages of each.

As you can see from figure 3.1, the questionnaire provides the most advantages. Since one of the disadvantages is that follow-up by telephone or face-to-face or small-group interviews may be necessary to ensure clarification or to obtain additional knowledge, it is recommended that you select the questionnaire approach augmented with

FIGURE 3.1 Comparison of Methods for Conducting a Job Analysis

Method	Description	Best for	Advantages	Disadvantages
Observation	Watching employees perform their job, recording tasks and duties observed, and then compiling information into the necessary skills, abilities, and knowledge	Repetitious, manual jobs	Simple	May not provide sufficient information, time-consuming, costly, requires an observation protocol, requires trained observers
Interview	Face-to-face discussion in which an employee is questioned about the skills, abilities, and knowledge needed to perform the job	Management jobs, any job that has changed markedly, and jobs where there is a difference between the employee's and supervisor's perception of the position	Thorough; increases involvement and input of interviewed employees	Time-consuming, expensive, may be redundant if many incumbents in the same job are interviewed
Questionnaire	Incumbents (and sometimes their managers) answer questions on a form outlining skills, abilities, and knowledge needed to perform the job; responses are compiled producing a composite statement of job requirements	Analyzing many jobs with limited human resources	Increases involvement as all employees complete the questionnaire; least expensive	May require follow-up for clarification
Work diaries or logs	Employee maintains an anecdotal record of the frequency and timing of tasks over an extended period of time; the information is reviewed to determine patterns	Most jobs	Thorough	Time-consuming and may not be easy to maintain; may require the diary to be kept over a long time to ensure that periodic (quarterly, annual) tasks are included

interviews as necessary. Because the questionnaire method will give you the most information over the widest variety of positions in a short time and because it is cost-effective, the job analysis questionnaire is fully discussed in this chapter. If you decide to add other methods, such as collecting logs or work diaries or observing work, you can easily add them.

Job Analysis Questionnaire

You, the members of the committee, or a member of the human resources department can draft a job analysis questionnaire (JAQ) to suit your needs. Suggested topics to include in the questionnaire are found in the following pages. In addition, figure 3.2 is a sample questionnaire that you may wish to adopt or use as a starting point for creating your own. The project manager and members of the committee should review the questionnaire after it is drafted. It should also be pilot tested by a cross section of employees (perhaps by a branch manager, circulation assistant, and library assistant). Feedback from the pilot test will alert you to language that might be vague or misunderstood. It will also help point out areas of inconsistency and redundancy or if the questions do not allow employees to completely describe their jobs. Based on this feedback, the JAQ should be revised as necessary before issuing it to all employees.

Topics

A sample JAQ is shown in figure 3.2. This sample is more appropriate if you are also planning to use the information for an internal equity job evaluation methodology, such as applying a point factor system to each job. (See chapter 6.) The items for which you will see information will reflect those factors important to, and valued by, your library system. They may include decision making, problem solving, communications, and customer service, to name a few.

For all purposes, in general the following topics should be covered in the questionnaire:

1. *Introduction and purpose* Include here a description of what this tool is and for what it will be used in addition to specific instructions for its completion. Also request the employee's name, title, place of work, length of time in current position, and part-time/full-time status. The length of time in the position helps to identify discrepancies that might be found between a relatively new employee and an experienced one in reporting position tasks. For example, it is possible that an incumbent with four months on the job is going to report a difference in duties and amount of time spent on each when compared with the incumbent with five years in the role. On the other end of the longevity spectrum, it is not necessarily true that the report of the experienced employee is more accurate. It is possible that the veteran may be performing functions that are now obsolete or that have emerged as functions of institutional knowledge or that the veteran

simply knows the job very well and handles it in an exemplary fashion. The point is—don't prejudge accuracy of responses based on longevity.

2. *Job summary or overview* Provide space for employees to include a brief narrative summary (3 to 4 sentences) of their position. (See part I of figure 3.2.) It might help if employees think of how they would describe to a friend what it is that they do on their jobs.

3. *Essential functions* Here, employees list those primary functions—performed on a regular basis—that make up the job, including duties and responsibilities that "define" the job without which the job could not be properly performed. (See part II of figure 3.2.) Duties equaling less than 5 percent of the job on a regular basis should not be included in this section. Essential functions are also critical to meet Americans with Disabilities Act (ADA) requirements, because these are the functions that an incumbent must be able to perform to fill this position. (There is more on ADA requirements later in this chapter.)

4. *Other functions* Employees should list additional or subsidiary functions that may be performed but are not essential to the job. These may also include special projects (part III of figure 3.2) or functions performed very rarely in terms of the entire scope of the position.

5. *Education* Employees check off a box corresponding to the level of education required for the position. This and the next section are often difficult for the employees in that they must remove their own individual qualifications from the picture and think about what is required to effectively perform the job. For example, a library clerk may have a bachelor's degree, but this degree was not required for the person to be hired for the job. Ask employees to check the *one* box that is the closest match. Note that it's not always possible to write a questionnaire that has an exact match in every category for every employee. (See part IV of figure 3.2.)

6. *Experience* Employees check off the box corresponding to the appropriate amount of experience required for the job. (See part V of figure 3.2.)

FIGURE 3.2   Sample Job Analysis Questionnaire

INTRODUCTION

The purpose of this questionnaire is to gather information about your job. We are asking you to complete the questionnaire because *you* know the most about *your* job. Your answers, the responses from other employees performing similar work, and your supervisor's comments will serve as the basis for

- summarizing key position information
- ensuring that all jobs are accurately assessed
- determining how jobs within the library compare with each other

**Remember to complete the questionnaire with *your job* in mind,
not your personal characteristics or performance.**

GENERAL INSTRUCTIONS

Before you begin to answer the questions, please take a few minutes to read through the entire questionnaire, reading all instructions carefully. Once you begin to answer the questions, be as objective as possible, responding about your job and *not* your personal situation or performance.

As you respond to the questions, your answers should reflect

what would normally be expected of someone fully trained in the job, rather than a beginner or someone performing over and above what is required

the expected or normal routine of the job rather than special projects, temporary assignments, or out-of-the-ordinary occurrences

the job as it is today, rather than what you expect it to become in the future

In addition:

Complete each section **accurately** and **thoroughly.** Try not to understate or inflate your answers. Please do not use acronyms or abbreviations.

Choose the **best** response for your job. If no response exactly matches your job, choose the **one** that reflects your job 90 percent or more of the time.

Answer **every** question.

Provide examples.

Feel free to write comments in any section and to attach additional materials if necessary.

Employees in the same position may complete one Job Analysis Questionnaire together.

After you have completed this questionnaire, please give it to your supervisor by *(date)*. If you have any questions, please contact your supervisor or one of the following members of the review committee:

Thank you for your participation.

(Signed)

Name: _____

Job Title: _____

Work Location: _____

How long in current position: _____

☐ Full-time position ☐ Part-time position

I. POSITION SUMMARY

Please provide a brief summary of your position.

HELPFUL TIPS

Think about how you would describe your job if a friend were to ask you what you do.
    You may wish to complete this section after you have completed the rest of the
questionnaire.

_____

_____

_____

_____

_____

_____

_____

_____

_____

_____

_____

_____

_____

_____

_____

_____

_____

_____

_____

_____

_____

(Continued)

FIGURE 3.2 **Sample Job Analysis Questionnaire** *(Continued)*

II. DUTIES AND RESPONSIBILITIES

Please describe the primary duties and responsibilities of your job **in order of importance.**

These statements should reflect the scope of your position under typical circumstances.

Consider your work assignments over a long enough period of time to picture your job as a whole. For instance, if your work varies from season to season or at specific times, you may have to view your job over an entire year to accurately estimate percentages. On the other hand, if your duties are basically the same from month to month, you may only have to consider your job over a week or month to accurately reflect percentages.

Generally, any activity that requires less than 5 percent of your time over the course of the year would not be listed unless it is a critical aspect of your work. For these duties you can use more-general terms and combine all or some of them to estimate a percentage.

Task	*Percentage*
1.	
2.	
3.	
4.	
5.	
6.	
7.	
8.	
Total	**100%**

III. SPECIAL PROJECTS

Please describe any special projects or assignments you are working on. Include an estimated duration or time frame for each (i.e., three months, summer, etc.) in the column on the right.

Project	Duration

IV. EDUCATION/TRAINING

This factor is an indication of the **minimal** education and training required to adequately perform the duties of your job. Select the minimum level of training or education that best describes the **job requirements** rather than your personal background. Please check only **one** box.

- ☐ a. My job requires less than a high school diploma but does require *some* training.
- ☐ b. My job requires a G.E.D. or a high school diploma.
- ☐ c. My job requires up to one year of job-related course work after high school.
- ☐ d. My job requires an associate's degree or two years of formal training beyond high school.
- ☐ e. My job requires a bachelor's degree.
- ☐ f. My job requires additional education in a specialized area.
- ☐ g. My job requires a master's degree.

V. EXPERIENCE

Please indicate the **minimum** level of relevant experience required to successfully perform your job. Please check only **one** box.

- ☐ a. No previous experience required
- ☐ b. 6 months–1 year experience
- ☐ c. 1–3 years' experience
- ☐ d. 3–5 years' experience
- ☐ e. 5–7 years' experience
- ☐ f. 7–10 years' experience
- ☐ g. More than 10 years' experience

(Continued)

FIGURE 3.2 **Sample Job Analysis Questionnaire** *(Continued)*

VI. CUSTOMER RELATIONS

Please provide information about the nature and extent of your regular contact and interaction with customers. Customers include internal customers, defined as other library employees, vendors, or contractors, or external customers, defined as those who use the library's services.

This question focuses upon the type of interaction the position has with customers as well as with the level of responsibility for customer satisfaction. Please check the **one box** that identifies the level of customer relations generally required in your job. You should report all contacts that are required on a regular basis.

☐ a. My work requires understanding and communicating routine, work-related information and requires normal courtesy and tact in dealing with others.

☐ b. My work requires understanding and communicating moderately complex information and identifying and resolving routine problems to ensure that customer satisfaction and service are maintained through daily interactions with internal and external contacts.

☐ c. My work requires understanding and communicating complex information or resolving complex problems; the job includes some accountability for ensuring customer satisfaction within the assigned area.

☐ d. My work requires persuading or gaining cooperation and acceptance of ideas and/or the resolution and/or negotiation of conflicts; the job has significant accountability for ensuring customer satisfaction within the branch or department.

☐ e. My work requires supporting controversial positions or negotiating sensitive issues; the job includes responsibility for monitoring and establishing business procedures to ensure customer service and satisfaction.

Please provide examples of the customer relations activities involved in your job.

_____

_____

_____

_____

_____

_____

_____

_____

_____

_____

_____

_____

VII. SUPERVISION

A. Supervisory Responsibility

Please check the **one** box that best describes the supervisory responsibility of your position.

☐ a. I have *no responsibility* for the direction of others.

☐ b. I am a *lead worker* performing essentially the same work as those supervised. I may assist in training.

☐ c. I *supervise* work within a unit or agency. I make recommendations on hiring and disciplinary actions. I evaluate program/work objectives and effectiveness and realign work as needed.

☐ d. I am responsible for training, instructing, and scheduling work within a unit or agency. I may have input into performance evaluations.

☐ e. I have direct responsibility for *supervising and managing* a department or unit's strategic work objectives and *assist* in resolving the most-complex problems.

☐ f. I *direct supervisors* in overseeing multiple work functions within the unit or agency. I make recommendations on hiring and disciplinary actions. I evaluate work objectives and effectiveness and recommend modifications to staffing patterns as needed.

☐ g. I have direct responsibility for *supervising and managing* the operations of *multiple departments* and resolve the most-complex problems.

B. Number Supervised

Please indicate the **number of employees** who report directly and indirectly to you. (Indirects are those who report through another supervisor or manager.)

	Full-Time	*Part-Time*
Direct		
Indirect		
Volunteer		

List the titles of all employees who report directly to you.

_____

_____

_____

_____

_____

_____

(Continued)

FIGURE 3.2   Sample Job Analysis Questionnaire *(Continued)*

C. Supervision Received

This factor measures the degree to which your immediate supervisor influences work activities of the position. The job's freedom to act and latitude in making policy, procedural, and daily operational decisions should be considered in responding to this question. Check the **one** box that best describes the supervision you receive in the position.

☐ a. My work is performed under general supervision, but I function independently on routine work; questionable cases and situations are referred to the immediate supervisor.

☐ b. My work is performed under general supervision with little functional guidance; I rarely refer cases to a supervisor unless a change to policy or procedure is involved.

☐ c. My work is performed under general direction; I use a wide range of procedures in meeting job responsibilities. I plan and arrange my own work and refer only unusual cases to supervision.

☐ d. My work is performed under broad administrative direction; I set forth standards for a department or division; I am directly accountable for results.

VIII. COMPLEXITY

Complexity identifies the extent to which your job requires that you perform varied activities and the amount of independent judgment you must use.

Please check the **one** box that best describes the most typical level of complexity of your job.

☐ a. My work duties are well defined with clearly stated directions or standards. My judgment is exercised on routine matters, and guidance is readily available.

☐ b. My work involves some nonroutine assignments that require new approaches or occasional independent judgment.

☐ c. My work involves moderately complicated procedures and tasks requiring independent judgment to select options and/or evaluate results.

☐ d. My work is complex and varied. It requires selection and application of technical or detailed skills in a variety of situations. A considerable degree of independent judgment is required.

☐ e. My work is extremely complex and varied. It requires a complete knowledge of a wide variety of operations and practices. It may require interaction with a number of others, teams, or departments to achieve success. I consistently use independent judgment.

Please provide an example of the complexity of your job.

_____

_____

_____

IX. DECISION MAKING

This question is in two parts. The first relates to decision-making **authority** and the second to the **impact** of the decisions made.

1. Authority (Check only **one** box.)

What decision-making **authority** exists in your job?

☐ a. I have the authority to *make routine or recurring decisions* or suggestions based on *rules or procedures.*

☐ b. I *consult with my supervisor or others before making nonroutine decisions* and share responsibility for the decisions.

☐ c. I *consult with others* on very difficult decisions and *share responsibility* for decisions.

☐ d. I *provide final approval* on decisions that affect my department or area of responsibility. I provide input on library policy decisions.

☐ e. I participate in decisions about *organization policy and strategy* or about significant transactions.

Please give a specific example.

_____

_____

2. Impact (Check only **one** box.)

What is the **impact** of the decisions you make on library operations?

☐ a. My incorrect decisions would affect primarily my own work, are easily detected, and have little impact.

☐ b. My poor or incorrect decisions may cause short delays in getting the work done in my area and affect other employees or library customers.

☐ c. My errors or poor decisions may cause major delays or disruptions to a library service or project.

☐ d. My errors or incorrect decisions may result in injury, damage to property or the library's reputation, or financial loss.

☐ e. My incorrect decisions would have an impact on systemwide plans and policies and may have a significant impact on the organization over the long term.

Please give a specific example.

_____

_____

(Continued)

FIGURE 3.2 **Sample Job Analysis Questionnaire** *(Continued)*

X. WORKING CONDITIONS

Working conditions are described as the physical effort required to perform the duties of the job and the environmental conditions under which the job duties are typically performed.

1. Physical Effort

Check the **one** box that best describes the physical effort demanded by the job.

☐ a. My work requires no unusual demand for physical effort.

☐ b. My work requires light physical effort in the handling of light materials or boxes and tools or equipment of up to 30 pounds in nonstrenuous work positions and/or continual standing or walking at least 60 percent of the time.

☐ c. My work demands occasional strenuous effort. For example, I have to handle moderately heavy boxes, moderately heavy tools, equipment, or materials of 30 to 60 pounds.

☐ d. My work requires constant physical effort including some lifting or handling of moderately heavy to heavy tools or materials of 60 pounds or more.

2. Environmental Factors

Check the **one** box that best describes the environmental factors of the job.

☐ a. The work environment involves everyday risks or discomforts that require normal safety precautions typical of such places as offices, meeting and training rooms, libraries, and residences or commercial vehicles, e.g., use of safe workplace practices with office equipment, avoidance of trips and falls, observance of fire regulations and traffic signals, and/or working in moderate outdoor weather conditions.

☐ b. The work involves risks or discomforts that require special safety precautions, e.g., working around moving parts, carts, or machines and/or working in adverse weather conditions.

XI. SUPERVISOR'S COMMENTS

This portion of the questionnaire is to be completed by your supervisor.

As a supervisor, it is important that you review this questionnaire and identify any discrepancies between the employee's responses and your own knowledge of the job. Remember, this questionnaire is intended solely for the purpose of accurately describing the position and **not the individual or his or her performance.**

If you would like to add a note or suggest a correction to any answer, please do so next to the employee's answer and identify your entry with your printed initials, without changing the employee's answer.

In addition, please complete the following:

1. Do you agree with the answers provided by the employee? If not, please explain.

2. List any important job duties this person performs that may have been omitted. Please add them under the appropriate section as well.

3. Additional comments:

Supervisor's name   Supervisor's title

_____   _____

Supervisor's signature   Date

_____   _____

7. *Customer relations* Customer relations are increasingly important in the library world. Employees check the box that most closely describes their customer service responsibilities. (See part VI of figure 3.2.)

8. *Supervision* This section may cover several subtopics: the level of supervision that is required for this position, the level of supervision this position provides, and the number of employees supervised. Employees may check off boxes but are also provided with space to provide relevant examples. (See part VII of figure 3.2.) This is important in that, again, employees feel heard and have been given ample opportunities to describe their jobs.

9. *Working and environmental conditions* Employees check off boxes relating to the amount and type of physical effort required to do the job as well as the type of working environment in which the job is performed, i.e., normal office conditions versus working outdoors in adverse weather. (See part X of figure 3.2.)

Respondents

It is important to send the questionnaire to all rather than a sample of employees. Although this adds time and cost to the project (including paper and copying costs as well as the extra time for employees to complete and management to review each questionnaire), it does, in fact, increase involvement. It allows all members of your workforce to have input into the process and to "be heard" about their jobs. Many employees are delighted to be given the opportunity to share information about their jobs with others—even in a written format. In fact, this may be the first time many employees have been asked to think about, reflect upon, and document their job duties. Sometimes the job descriptions for the library's positions are woefully out of date—sometimes to the point of being completely obsolete. The information gathered from the questionnaires will provide details about current job duties and responsibilities—and will also supply an impetus for you to update your system's job descriptions at the end of the compensation study.

Although some colleagues may disagree, employees in the same position should complete the questionnaire as a group. This supports the concept of teamwork, and employees find it more interesting by learning more about their organization as a whole and their department or position from the process. This collaborative approach also cuts down on the volume of paperwork and supervisory review. Group completion also helps minimize embarrassment if an employee has problems with reading and writing to complete the questionnaire. A group should only complete the questionnaire if all members are performing essentially the same tasks. Differences, if any, should be noted. There may be situations where several employees share the same title but are, for one reason or another, performing different jobs. In these cases you may need to offer guidance to groups of employees who complete questionnaires together.

Employees should supply examples or attach any additional information that they believe will help explain their jobs. While attachments are more rare than commonplace, employees have taken the liberty to provide everything from a chart of accounts to a five-page recitation of daily activities—in five-minute increments. Employees may attach examples of reports, spreadsheets, or other documents they've developed or produced. Some employees have even attached T-shirts, bookmarks, and other marketing materials they developed. This information occasionally adds to an understanding of the employee's tasks and activities. Although it will not substantially affect your understanding of the job, allowing the employees to attach this information creates more buy-in, and they appreciate the opportunity to share something about their jobs. This indeed is an important reason by itself to encourage the attachments.

Kick-off Meeting and Instructions

When possible, invite all employees involved in the study to a communications meeting before they complete the questionnaire. This meeting can be offered in several sessions if large numbers of employees are involved or if employees are at disparate locations. The meeting allows you the opportunity to describe project steps, discuss the employees' roles in the project, and give employees the opportunity to ask questions. Having a meeting of this type during the initial steps of the project sends quite a few important messages to employees. First, it lets them know that this is an open process—that the project steps aren't secrets. Employees often (and rightly so) feel nervous or apprehensive during compensation studies. They may worry about pay being cut or about losing their jobs. These communication sessions give you the chance to address those questions and concerns and to manage expectations.

The flip side of the anxiety that may be created by the project is the expectation that everyone will receive large pay raises. One way to allay these fears and manage expectations is to identify a set of related guidelines. For instance, the philosophy presented in this book is that no employee should lose pay or his or her job as a result of a compensation study. However, employees should not plan to book a Caribbean cruise or go on a shopping spree either. Explain that until the market review has been performed and the data analyzed, it is impossible to tell what the results of the study will indicate and how or if those findings can be implemented.

An additional benefit of having a kick-off meeting with employees is the opportunity to centrally distribute and review the questionnaire along with guidelines for its completion. Employees usually have many questions about the completion of the JAQ. Again, there is often some fear associated with "doing it wrong." It's important to explain that these questionnaires are an avenue for learning about the duties and responsibilities of the job and that their individual performance, skills, abilities, education, or experience are not at issue. It's hard to remove the individual employee from the job he or she performs, but that is exactly what must be done to get objective job content information.

Emphasize that employees filling out the questionnaire should evaluate what is really needed to do the job *by an average performer*—not a superstar, underachiever or overachiever, or new employee. Remind employees that you are looking for the minimum qualifications required for their specific jobs, not what they individually might possess

in terms of education, years of experience, etc. Nonetheless, and probably not surprisingly, employees may overexaggerate the requirements of the position or share *their* years of experience and education versus those required by the job. Conversely, employees may also underestimate the requirements of their jobs and check lower-level descriptions. For example, several library assistants indicated on their questionnaires that five years of experience and an MLS would be required to perform their job in a competent manner. In contrast, a branch manager stated that an associate's degree and two years' experience in business would fit the bill in finding the caliber of person who would enable the branch to run in an efficient and effective manner. Since the potential exists for both extremes, it is advisable and helpful to have a review by knowledgeable reviewers—experienced consultants if you are using them or members of a review team. Also especially helpful (although not always the definitive source) is supervisory review.

Allow employees to take up to two weeks to complete the questionnaire, and ask them to turn it in to their supervisor.

Confidentiality and the Questionnaire

Unlike an organizational or cultural assessment, the JAQ is not a confidential source document. It is designed to collect information about a job and requirements of an employee to perform it. The questionnaires will be reviewed by others, so be upfront with employees about that. In addition, if the job description writers or those evaluating the position need more information, they will need to return to respondents.

There is one exception to this statement about confidentiality—and it applies to only one part of the questionnaire. For example, in addition to a library system wanting its compensation and pay plan updated to reflect the market or internal equity, it may also want to design a performance management system, provide recommendations on library staffing and structure, or facilitate an organizational design process. To save time and costs, as well as to provide a quick preliminary overview of the issues at hand, an extra sheet could be added to the JAQ asking a variety of pertinent questions. For example, figure 3.3 shows confidential JAQ questions for a large urban library system that wanted to design optimal staffing levels for small branches, large branches, and the central (main) library departments. For an organizational redesign study designed for a small system neighboring a major metropolitan area, a confidential section was added to the JAQ, as shown in figure 3.4.

In both these instances a variety of options were provided to employees for returning the information in a confidential manner. Options included faxing, e-mailing, or mailing (anonymously) directly to the consultant. Employees were also told they could return this page with their questionnaire if they were comfortable with this option and chose to do so. Finally, the instructions reminded employees about the phase of the project that these

---

FIGURE 3.3   Confidential Questions on Staffing Levels

Name: (optional)_____   Department:_____

Position: _____

1. Are there any aspects of your job that you think you should be doing that you are not doing? If so, what and why?

2. Are there any aspects of your job that you really should not be doing because they do not provide a return to the library equal to your investment of time and effort, are not necessary, are repetitive, are outdated, are inefficient, etc.? If so, what and why?

3. Are there any ways you think the library could operate in a more efficient and effective manner? If so, what and how?

FIGURE 3.4   Confidential Questions for an Organizational Redesign Study

Name: (optional)_____   Department:_____

Position: _____

1. What are your department's goals? Are they being met? Please describe.

2. Does your department provide good customer service? Please describe.

3. Are there any aspects of your job that you think you should be doing that you are not now doing? If so, what and why?

4. Are there any aspects of your job that you really should not be doing because they do not provide a return equal to your investment of time and effort, are not necessary, are repetitive, are outdated, are inefficient, etc.? If so, what and why?

5. Do you feel you possess the appropriate skills for a changing work environment (i.e., knowledge of PC applications such as databases, Internet, etc.), or could you use some training in a specific area? If so, what type of training would be helpful?

6. Are there any ways you think the system could operate in a more efficient and effective manner? If so, what and how?

---

questions related to and stated that **"It is not necessary for supervisors to review or comment on these responses"** in bold letters. Note, however, that questions such as these may not be appropriate if the study is conducted by internal library personnel only because it may be difficult to ensure confidentiality.

These types of projects request only the employee's perceptions and comments. Employees' names must be optional, and all information must be kept confidential, with only summary findings reported. Expect to receive a very high rate of response on such addendums—in excess of 50 percent and often as high as 90 percent.

Supervisory Review

While parts I–X of the sample questionnaire in figure 3.2 are to be completed by the employee, part XI allows for a review by the employee's supervisor. The supervisor is asked not to make any changes to the JAQ but to provide comments. Here the supervisor can comment, for example, on whether the respondent may have overestimated or underestimated when responding to different sections.

Supervisors typically have one week to review the JAQs of the employees reporting directly to them. The amount of work involved for the supervisor, of course, depends on the size of the library system. In some library systems a second level of review also takes place, usually by the assistant director responsible for that area (e.g., public services or administration). In smaller library systems, the assistant director or library director may review all JAQs.

Having reviewed each questionnaire, if the supervisor disagrees with an employee's response to a certain question, he or she should initiate a conversation with that employee about the job in addition to providing comments on the JAQ itself. Oftentimes, jobs evolve in many small ways over a period of time. It is not unusual that the supervisor neither notices nor keeps track of all of the changes. In many cases, employees, and the responsibilities of their jobs, just grow over time. This is not at all unusual for library systems, which in recent years have seen check-out machines, vast changes in technology, outsourcing, fund-raising, restructuring,

customer demands, demographic changes, worker shortages, etc., playing prominent roles in day-to-day library life. It happens so often and so quickly that by the time one "formal" change might be made to a job or job description, it might be time to make another. Therefore, the job description should be reviewed by both the employee and supervisor on an annual basis, usually at the time of the annual performance review. Upon agreement, if warranted, it should be updated and submitted to the human resources department or other individual responsible for maintaining job descriptions.

Sorting Completed Questionnaires

Now that you have received all of these questionnaires from your employees and you have reviewed them—what's next? First, you should be aware that you probably will receive a very high return rate of questionnaires from employees—typically more than 95 percent. After the JAQs have been submitted to a central location (usually the human resources office or your designated project manager), the next step is to sort them by current position title, regardless of location, and by current salary grade. It is also advisable to separate branch positions from main library positions (if applicable). These may be combined later, but at this point it is important to see if there are any major differences in the scope or nature of the positions attributable to location or size. For example, you should sort all JAQs for circulation clerks in grade 2 assigned to the main library in a separate stack from the circulation clerks in the same grade who work in branch libraries. You should also separate positions that have more than one level; for instance, you may have two or three levels of branch managers or library assistants assigned to different grades. These should be separated as well.

Next, sort the questionnaires in order of current grade, lowest to highest. Having all of the JAQs sorted this way will allow you to go through them quickly and obtain an overview of the system, the positions in it, and the interdependencies among them. It also enables you to see any potential problem areas and highlights areas where more information is needed. Obviously, a person with sufficient knowledge of your system should do this sorting.

If you are a member of an internal project committee, you might want to form a subcommittee to perform this process and make it easier for the reviewers or your consultant. It will make your project go faster, and the cost will ultimately be lower than if you have a consultant because he or she will not have to struggle to figure out who's who.

It is strongly recommended that you make copies of your completed questionnaires before sending them on for review. You don't want to have to ask each employee to complete the questionnaires again if they should somehow get lost in the process.

A next step is to use the information gathered from the JAQs and employee interviews and prepare job summaries. (Job summaries are discussed in detail in chapter 4.)

Interviews with Employees

Even though the topic of conversation pertains to their jobs, another time that confidentiality must be ensured is when employees are interviewed. When designing a new compensation system, even when working with a steering or review team, it is often necessary to interview employees to learn more about their jobs.

After all JAQs are received, they should be reviewed with an eye for the following:

- unresolved disagreements between supervisor and employee perceptions of the job
- positions where employees who hold what appears to be the same position have widely different tasks
- where more information is necessary to fully understand the position

It is also necessary to identify jobs that have undergone significant changes, that have a significant rate of turnover, or that have not been reclassified for a long time even though there were requests to do so. Ultimately you should interview approximately 20 percent (depending upon the size of the library system and the feasibility of this task) of the employees. When there are multiple incumbents in a job title, they can be interviewed as a small group rather than in individual interviews. This process not only provides an even greater understanding of the job, it also involves more employees directly in the process, thereby enhancing their knowledge of how others do the job and fostering additional ownership and commitment to the project.

LEGAL COMPLIANCE

Your library's job descriptions (see chapter 4) must be in compliance with state and local legislation and with federal laws such as the Equal Employment Opportunity (EEO) Act, Pay Equity Analysis Act in Canada, and the Americans with Disabilities Act (ADA).

Effective July 1992, the ADA requires employers to identify "essential job functions." Essential job functions are those parts of a job that cannot be easily reassigned or delegated to another employee. That is, employees who do not have an impairment that would prevent them from doing so must perform these essential job functions. Once the essential functions are defined (via job analysis), you are required to make reasonable accommodations that will allow an otherwise qualified disabled person to perform the essential job functions. "Essential job functions" and "reasonable accommodations" have to be determined on a case-by-case basis. (The sample JAQ in figure 3.2 accounts for a delineation of "essential job functions" as well as working conditions.) There are many books and publications, as well as advice from your attorney, that can help you learn more about the ADA. This section is designed to give you an overview of your responsibilities in this area so that you can write job descriptions that are useful and in compliance.

You may be wondering if your library system is required to comply with the provisions of the ADA. The answer is probably yes. Title II extends the prohibition of discrimination on the basis of disability to all activities of state and local governments, including those that do not receive federal financial assistance. By law, Title II of the ADA covers programs, activities, and services of public entities. Public entities are defined as

> any state or local government
>
> any department, agency, special-purpose district, or other instrumentality of a state or local government
>
> certain commuter authorities as well as AMTRAK

Title II does not include the federal government, which is covered by sections 501 and 504 of the Rehabilitation Act of 1973. Title II is intended to apply to all programs, activities, and services provided or operated by state and local governments. Where it may be difficult to ascertain whether a library is in fact a public entity, as some appear to have both public and private features, review the following criteria with your attorney:

1. Is the library operated with public funds?
2. Are employees considered government employees?
3. Do you receive significant assistance from the government by provision of property or equipment?
4. Is the library governed by an independent board chosen by members of a private organization? By an elected board? Appointed by elected officials?

Experience indicates that all public libraries are public entities and are covered by the provisions of ADA. Academic libraries that are a part of a public institution of higher education and K–12 school libraries most likely need to comply with ADA as well. Private and special libraries should check their legal requirements under the ADA with their attorneys.

Definition of Essential Functions

According to the Equal Employment Opportunity Commission (EEOC) regulations implementing ADA, a job function may be considered essential if any of the following conditions exist:

> The position exists to perform that function.
>
> There are a limited number of available employees among whom the performance of that function can be distributed.
>
> The function is so highly specialized that the incumbent in the position was hired for his or her ability to perform that function.

The EEOC considers various forms of evidence when determining whether a particular function is essential. This evidence includes

> the judgment of the library director, assistant director, or senior human resources professional
>
> written job descriptions prepared *prior to* advertising or interviewing for the job
>
> the amount of time spent on the job performing that function
>
> the consequences to the functioning of the library system or to public service of not requiring the incumbent to perform the function
>
> if unionized, the provisions of a collective bargaining agreement
>
> work experience of prior employees in the job
>
> work experience of current employees in similar jobs within the library system

Consult with your attorney concerning other questions you might have about compliance with the ADA.

4
Job Descriptions

The information that has been collected via job analysis will be used in the preparation of your job descriptions. A job description is a summary of the most important features of the job. It identifies the job and describes the general nature of the work and specific tasks, responsibilities, outcomes, and competencies required to perform the job. Your objective is to provide enough information in a consistent format that summarizes job tasks in an accurate, clear, and useful way without being so specific as to limit the flexibility of the employee in the position or the flexibility of the position in your system. All parties—the employee, his or her supervisor, and your human resources professional—should have input into the process and reach consensus that the final job description is an accurate representation of the work being performed. Since job descriptions are often used during an external market analysis (see chapter 7), they should also provide enough information to ensure that the persons or firm conducting the study will be able to make high-quality job matches.

Before writing job descriptions, you should understand the components and decide whether you want to use generic or specific descriptions (discussed later in this chapter).

MULTIPURPOSE STUDIES

Nothing in the library stands alone—it's all part of a system. As mentioned earlier, consultants are often retained to work on an organization redesign, reengineering, or staffing and structure analysis simultaneously with a compensation study. But which should come first?

Without a doubt, studies involving strategic planning and process evaluation *should* come first. If the library system has a plan and knows where it is going based upon new technologies, changes in funding patterns, demographic shifts, or new or fewer services to the community, that knowledge should be the guide to designing or redesigning your jobs. The jobs might also need to be priced differently in the marketplace to reflect new duties and responsibilities or changes to them. For this reason, it is best to proceed in the following sequence:

- strategic planning
- organization design (to support the plan)
- staffing and structure analysis (including job design to support the organization design)
- job descriptions (or summaries) of the new or revised positions
- compensation system to attract and retain qualified staff
- pay for performance and bonus or incentive and other recognition programs to reward excellent performance and goal achievement

However logical and reasonable it would seem that the planning process should take place using the model outlined, it doesn't always happen that way. Often the library system starts with the compensation plan—largely because that's where the "pain" is strongest. The library system might be experiencing high turnover, an inability to recruit at all levels, or a feeling that employees are not paid in line with their recruitment market. Having a strategic plan is critical for a variety of reasons, but none is more important than having the ability to map out the work that needs to be accomplished to achieve your goals. This, in turn, will help you identify the skills that will be required of staff. Learn as much as you can about your future—what services you'll be expected to provide and what your staff will need to learn to provide those services—and incorporate that knowledge into your study.

Assuming you know what tasks you need your future or current employees to perform, there should be no problem market pricing your redesigned jobs even if the jobs are still evolving or don't yet exist. When the organization design project comes after the compensation study, it can ultimately cost your library more money. That is, the job descriptions you might have just approved will need to be redesigned and market-priced, and adjustments to some employees' salaries might also be warranted. The key is to deal with the issues as quickly as pos-

sible and communicate revisions or updates to all employees so they know what is happening and why.

HOW TO DRAFT THE JOB DESCRIPTION

The easiest way to draft the job description is to use the information obtained in job analysis and an appropriate template. The job analysis questionnaire completed by employees and reviewed by supervisors offers a wealth of information about each job. Drafting job descriptions is the first place to capitalize on this information. Worksheet 6 includes two templates for job descriptions that you can choose from to adapt and customize for your use. All you need to do now is to group the job descriptions according to title and complete each template by filling in the components (explained in the following sections). The job description should be drafted and submitted to the supervisor and to human resources for review. It is prudent to obtain employee sign-off as well, to ensure accuracy from their perspective as well as to promote commitment and buy-in.

Often consultants perform the task of writing descriptions. Alternatively, an individual from the human resources department may undertake this assignment, or it could be a function of the compensation committee.

Job Description Components

Regardless of the format you select, job descriptions typically include the following components:

job summary a brief description that summarizes the overall purpose and objectives of the position and the results the employee is expected to accomplish; some include the amount and the degree of freedom or independence the employee has to act or the name of the position to which a person holding this job reports

essential functions the tasks, duties, and responsibilities of the position that are most important to get the job done; required to comply with the ADA

additional or nonessential functions the desirable but not absolutely necessary aspects of the job and the job duties for which accommodation can reasonably be made

knowledge, skills, and abilities the specific minimum competencies required for job performance: *knowledge* is the body of information, such as library science one has acquired; *skills* include problem solving, communicating orally, and the like; *abilities* are those personal characteristics an employee has that may be necessary to excel on the job, such as the ability to make decisions or effectively supervise others

supervisory responsibilities (sometimes included in job descriptions) the scope of the position's authority, including a list of jobs that report to the incumbent (It may be better to make references to "assigned staff" in lieu of specific position titles, as these would have to be changed every time a structural, staffing, or organizational change takes place.)

working conditions the environment in which the job is performed, especially any unique conditions beyond those found in a normal office or library environment; in conjunction with the essential functions, required by the ADA

minimum qualifications minimum (as well as desired, but you must include the minimum) educational requirements, experience, and licenses required to perform the job

Worksheet 6 contains the preceding components in template A. Another format for job descriptions is shown in template B.

The Language of Job Descriptions

When writing job descriptions, the language should be consistent among all jobs in your system. Use action verbs with an implied subject (that is, the *who* implied is the holder of the position) and explicit outputs (the *what* of the job). For example:

   evaluates children's literature

labels and processes materials

supervises assigned staff

assists patrons with locating materials and information using electronic and online databases and resources

performs circulation tasks including registering patrons, checking materials in and out, and answering questions regarding library policies

develops departmental goals and objectives

Furthermore, consider this tip from the director of an academic library: "Be smart," she said, "in how you write job descriptions and the language you use." In her world, job descriptions go through the university's human resources department for approval and grade assignments. She suggested the use of the right terminology when writing them, especially when they involve information technology skills. What is the right terminology? The right terminology is what the rest of the university (or, if you are a public library, the county) is using when evaluating its information technology jobs. For example, if the librarian is managing an integrated library system (having, of course, many complex records, etc.), write that the job is database manager. Use the words "systems," "Web master," "technical trainer," and so forth when describing the duties of the members of your workforce. They are likely to be more highly compensated that way.

Broad versus Specific Job Descriptions

Should job descriptions be broad or specific? In other words, how much detail should be included? An example of the type of flexibility referred to is for a manager to be empowered to ask a "clerical assistant grade 2," who spends most of her time checking books in and out, to help out in the materials processing department, where there is a vacancy for someone at the grade 2 level. A library system that has broad job descriptions would call a position "clerical assistant" or "library assistant" with possible duties including checking books in and out, processing books, aiding customers by

Basic Job Description Forms

TEMPLATE A

Job title: _____ Salary range: _____

Department: _____ Reports to: _____

Position Summary: _____

_____

_____

Essential functions: Percentage of time
                                                            spent on each:

1. _____

   _____   _____%

2. _____

   _____   _____%

3. _____

   _____   _____%

4. _____

   _____   _____%

Other functions:

1. _____

   _____

2. _____

   _____

3. _____

   _____

Minimum Job Requirements:

   Education: _____

   Experience: _____

   Specific skills:_____

   Specialized knowledge, licenses, etc.:_____

   Supervisory responsibility, if any: _____

   _____

   Working conditions: _____

   _____

(Continued)

TEMPLATE B

1. **Who?** (the position or incumbent) _____

2. Does **what** work? (including review of others' work) _____
   _____
   _____

   a. essential _____
      _____
      _____

   b. nonessential_____
      _____
      _____

3. **Where?** _____

4. **When?** (or how often) _____

5. **Why?** (purpose or impact of work) _____

6. **How** is work accomplished? _____

troubleshooting computer problems, counting money, record keeping, filing, receiving and checking in shipments of materials, having familiarity with the library's automated circulation system, and so forth. A library system with specific job descriptions and titles would refer to that same position as two separate positions: circulation clerk and materials processor; persons holding either of these positions would rarely fill in or help out the other's departments.

While little that's been said so far about job descriptions is controversial, this is one area where some human resources professionals disagree. However, I favor broad job descriptions for a variety of reasons.

First, library systems are constantly undergoing change and transition. New technologies, flattened job hierarchies, networked communications, and increased responsibility for decision making to promote high levels of customer service are a way of life in today's libraries. These trends probably will not stabilize or slow down in the near future. Therefore, broad job descriptions provide some flexibility in the roles employees play and the tasks they need to accomplish.

Second, the labor market at the time of this writing is very tight for many of the jobs in library systems. This probably will not change either. Managers and supervisors need flexibility to assign employees appropriately to accomplish necessary tasks. Of course, care should be taken to ensure that new work assignments are reviewed carefully and that a similar type, level, or complexity of work should be assigned to an employee in a given salary grade. If an employee is consistently assigned lower- or higher-level duties, that employee's position should be reevaluated.

Third, while this might be implied already, job descriptions that are too narrow can serve as a roadblock or bottleneck to making changes or meeting customer needs (i.e., "It's not my job"). Even though many job descriptions have disclaimers, an employee may view the description as all-encompassing. Obviously, this can cause employee relations issues if not resolved early on.

Fourth, job descriptions that are very specific can become out-of-date before the ink is dry. Keeping them current can be a full-time job. With the myriad of technological changes presenting themselves to library staff each day, it is impractical to list—and therefore limit yourself to—every electronic database or Internet search tool a librarian may need to use. Keep these statements broad, and you'll also save time by not having to constantly revise job descriptions. For example, some library systems assign positions to a specific branch. In some locations, that really ties the library director's hands when it comes to optimizing staffing patterns or indeed providing for development opportunities and cross training for incumbents. One option is to include a disclaimer (discussed in a following section) that states that "all positions are eligible for systemwide transfer."

Fifth, library systems should think about the degree to which they need employees who are technical specialists versus generalists when making hiring decisions. This does not refer to the dreaded "g" word (generalism) that five years ago made a public library client quake (although that client is now leaning more in that direction with some branches having full-service desks serving all customers, adults and children alike, from one desk using the same librarians). That is, generalists are flexible employees who can float into various departments, handle a variety of tasks, and tackle special assignments.

Finally, as education stimulates the growth of new skills and abilities, many employees enjoy being flexible and having an opportunity to try out their new learnings. Some enjoy and thrive on it for its own sake; others value it because they know it makes them more marketable.

Given the economic pressures of rapid organizational and technological change, fiscal conservatism of local governments, increased competition, and the customer's demands for fine-tuned customer service, job descriptions need to allow for broader—not more limiting—application. Some may resist this idea because people don't like to change. Employees like knowing what to do, and some may have difficulty handling ambiguity. Clear communication and training are the answers to ensure that employees are comfortable handling new assignments. Once-skeptical employees turn into advocates after reaching a comfort level with a new task, process, or technology.

Many supervisors find it more difficult to manage in this environment. It is far easier to manage in accordance with a clearly delineated document that specifies what employees should do and how they should do it. It is actually harder to give employees the freedom and flexibility needed to do their work to meet today's challenges. This type of flexibility is being demanded by the GenXers who are becoming increasingly represented in our employee populations.

Customizing Job Descriptions

Customize job descriptions in accordance with your needs. Peter Vaill, an expert in organizational development and change management, popularized the concept of "permanent white water" in his book *Managing as a Performing Art.*[1] This phrase characterizes a work environment that doesn't fit into the old model of change with its inherent uncertainty followed by a longer period of adjustment and stability. Instead, in a state of "permanent white water," one major change is followed by another, and so on. The periods of calm between the turmoil don't seem to exist for many in the work world today. If you're working in such an environment, fluid, flexible job descriptions are essential. If your library or system is smaller and more stable, perhaps more content-specific job descriptions would be appropriate.

In a recent experience with a suburban public library system with eight branches, the library wanted to promote certain values and behaviors that were important to the system. Figure 4.1 shows what they incorporated into *each* job description under the essential functions section.

Another forward-thinking system developed sets of behaviors for each library position that were used

FIGURE 4.1   Essential Job Functions for All Jobs at XYZ Library

Serves on branch or system committees and participates in workshops, seminars, and training as requested

Notifies the supervisor with suggested ways to improve the efficiency and effectiveness of personnel and procedures and systemwide goals and objectives

Maintains good public relations with the community through contacts with public officials, community leaders, Friends of the Library, appropriate school personnel, and the general public

Learns new skills and technologies to retain proficiency in areas of expertise

Is dependable and punctual

Maintains a positive, friendly, and cooperative attitude and provides consistent customer service

Upholds all library policies and procedures as defined in the library's *Policies and Procedures Manual*

Completes time sheet and other necessary forms and reports accurately and in a timely manner

In addition to the specific duties and responsibilities of this job, it is the responsibility of every employee to comply with the library's values statement, customer service guidelines, and all other policies detailed in the *Employee Handbook* and *Policies and Procedures Manual.*

---

as part of the performance management process. They, in turn, included references to these sets of behaviors in the job descriptions, thus creating consistency and accountability in the overall compensation and classification systems. These job descriptions included statements such as the following:

trains, coaches, and evaluates staff in information service behaviors, collection development and maintenance procedures, programming techniques, and other areas as necessary

greets customers and responds to reference and reader's advisory requests using model reference and reader's advisory behaviors

Job descriptions can—and should—be tailored to fit the needs, expectations, and culture of your library system.

Disclaimers

Although using generic job descriptions is highly recommended, there is no way around dealing with the infamous "other duties as assigned" section. Regardless of how broad your library's job descriptions will be, they still must contain enough information to add value. No longer can we look at a five-year-old job description and assume it is still accurate. As you read this, you may feel this way

about some of your job descriptions that are just two or three years old.

To remind employees and supervisors alike that job descriptions are subject to change and that they are not meant to be all-inclusive, consider adding—or customizing—one of the following disclaimers.

The above job description is not intended as, nor should it be construed as, exhaustive of all responsibilities, skills, efforts, or working conditions associated with this job. Reasonable accommodations may be made to enable qualified individuals with disabilities to perform the essential functions of this job. This and all library positions are eligible for systemwide transfer.

Management reserves the right to assign or reassign duties and responsibilities at any time.

This job description reflects the current essential functions of this position; it is understood that other tasks or duties may be assigned as the work environment dictates.

Features of this job are described below. Job duties and tasks may be subject to change at any time due to reasonable accommodation or other reasons.

Figures 4.2–4.4 show sample completed job descriptions with disclaimers.

FIGURE 4.2   Sample Job Description: Library Clerk

Date: 5/02

Job Summary

Performs a variety of routine clerical tasks to support library operations; performs other duties as assigned

Essential Functions

1. Answer phones, greet and direct customers to appropriate areas
2. May
   a. perform circulation duties such as checking materials in and out, registering customers for library cards, providing orientation to library use, and calculating and collecting fines and fees
   b. assist customers by locating and retrieving materials and demonstrating and providing instruction in the use of library equipment, including computers
   c. reshelve materials and revise shelves as needed
   d. process ILL requests, holds for customers, and orders for materials
   e. perform clerical duties such as typing, filing, copying, or sorting and distributing mail
   f. calculate and maintain daily, monthly, and yearly statistics
   g. maintain, order, and receive supplies from vendors and distribute to branches and departments
   h. strip, clean, and process a/v materials and containers for reuse
   i. send old magazines to be bound for library's collection
   j. open and/or close branch
3. Perform other duties as assigned

Required Knowledge, Skills, and Abilities

1. Ability to
   a. gain working knowledge of the library's policies and procedures
   b. act as a representative of the library to the public
   c. learn the current shelving system
   d. learn to operate relevant computer systems, including hardware and software, and simple office machines
2. Knowledge of basic math skills

Education and Experience

1. High school diploma or G.E.D.
2. Six months to one year of related experience or equivalent technical training, education, or experience

Physical and Environmental Conditions

1. Work requires no unusual demand for physical effort
2. Work environment involves everyday risks or discomforts that require normal safety precautions typical of such places as offices or meeting rooms, e.g., use of safe workplace practices with office equipment and avoidance of trips and falls

This job description is not intended as, nor should it be construed as, exhaustive of all responsibilities, skills, efforts, or working conditions associated with this job.

Reasonable accommodations may be made to enable qualified individuals with disabilities to perform the essential functions of this job.

This and all library positions are eligible for system-wide transfer.

EMPLOYEE AND SUPERVISORY REVIEW AND BUY-IN

After collecting information on each of your jobs and writing the job descriptions, you will have plenty of information to begin a compensation study; however, there is one step remaining: employee and supervisory review. When job descriptions are still in draft format, make certain that employees and their supervisors have an opportunity to review them. Allowing all constituencies input into the process is beneficial for a variety of reasons, including helping to ensure that you have captured the essence of the position without missing any relevant duties or tasks, providing supervisors and all employees with a document they can "live with," and promoting employee and supervisory buy-in of the job descriptions themselves and

FIGURE 4.3   Sample Job Description: Library Assistant, Technical Services

Date: 5/02

Job Summary

Performs a variety of clerical duties related to the acquisition, receiving, and processing of library materials including, but not limited to, placing orders for a variety of materials, data entry related to orders, and creating item records for all formats of material; performs other duties as assigned

Essential Functions

1. Place online orders from selection lists for all types of library materials, including books, videos, CDs, audio-cassettes, etc., using the library's automated program
2. Pull purchase orders and enter data related to orders on the automated program
3. Create item records for all formats of material
4. Process/package all formats of material
5. Obtain price and availability information via various electronic resources
6. Enter data for each order on an Excel spreadsheet
7. Maintain and update supplier lists
8. Create new supplier records in automated system
9. Perform serial checks for current and new magazine subscriptions using automated system
10. Rectify orders and activity logs
11. Manage the process for returning materials, copying, packaging, etc.
12. Check acknowledgment notices for unavailable books and notify materials assistants of same
13. Call vendors to check on overdue orders
14. Edit item records or individual copies
15. Distribute material for delivery to branches
16. Repair, repackage, or transfer material
17. Withdraw materials following established procedures
18. Refer questions to appropriate inter- and intradepartment staff
19. Provide assistance to acquisitions and cataloging staff as directed
20. Serve on branch or system committees and participate in workshops, seminars, and training as requested
21. Notify the branch manager with suggested ways to improve the efficiency and effectiveness of personnel and procedures and systemwide goals and objectives
22. Maintain good public relations with the community through contacts with public officials, community leaders, Friends of the Library, appropriate school personnel, and the general public
23. Learn new skills and technologies to retain proficiency in areas of expertise
24. Be dependable and punctual
25. Maintain a positive, friendly, and cooperative attitude and provide consistent customer service
26. Uphold all library policies and procedures as defined in the library's *Policies and Procedures Manual*
27. Complete time sheet and other necessary forms and reports accurately and in a timely manner
28. Perform other duties as assigned

In addition to the specific duties and responsibilities of this job, it is the responsibility of every employee to comply with the library's values statement, customer service guidelines, and all other policies detailed in the *Employee Handbook* and *Policies and Procedures Manual.*

Required Knowledge, Skills, and Abilities

1. Ability to gain working knowledge of library policies and procedures
2. Ability to act as a representative of the library to the public
3. Knowledge of technical services policies and procedures
4. Ability to learn to maintain and organize library materials
5. Ability to prepare and maintain accurate records
6. Ability to learn to operate relevant computer systems, including hardware and software, and office machines
7. Strong communication skills, both verbal and written
8. Basic math and language skills

Education and Experience

1. High school diploma or G.E.D.
2. Six months or more related experience

Physical and Environmental Conditions

1. Work requires light physical effort in the handling of light materials up to 30 pounds in nonstrenuous work positions or continual standing or walking 60 percent or more of the time
2. Work environment involves everyday risks or discomforts that require normal safety precautions typical of such places as offices or meeting rooms, e.g., use of safe workplace practices with office equipment and avoidance of trips and falls

This job description is not intended as, nor should it be construed as, exhaustive of all responsibilities, skills, efforts, or working conditions associated with this job.

Reasonable accommodations may be made to enable qualified individuals with disabilities to perform the essential functions of this job.

This and all library positions are eligible for system-wide transfer.

FIGURE 4.4   Sample Job Description: Librarian

Position number:

Date: 3/02

Job Summary

Assists customers in locating and using the available resources of the library and provides timely and accurate information and answers to research questions; selects/orders specific materials as directed; performs other duties as assigned

Essential Functions

1. Provide reference assistance to customers and library staff in person, by phone, and via e-mail including explaining the arrangement of the library, identifying the types of materials available, guiding users to sources of information, providing instruction in the use of various library reference sources, and contacting external experts

2. Assist with collection development, maintenance, and management in assigned area

3. Participate in library projects, committees, and activities as assigned

4. May support community outreach programs including library tours and participation in community organizations

5. May specialize in a particular area such as children's materials, periodicals, reference, media, business and technology, or other specialty and may serve as in-house expert in assigned area

6. May recruit, train, and supervise library employees and volunteers

7. May be located in the central library or a branch

8. Perform other duties as instructed and assigned

Required Knowledge, Skills, and Abilities

1. May require knowledge of specialty subject area

2. Good interpersonal, communication, and organizational skills

3. Research skills including online database searching

4. Ability to use relevant library hardware, software, and other equipment

Education and Experience

1. Master's in Library Science

2. No previous experience required

3. Or equivalent technical training, education, and/or experience

Physical and Environmental Conditions

1. Work requires light physical effort in the handling of light materials or boxes and tools or equipment up to 30 pounds in nonstrenuous work positions and/or continual standing or walking 60 percent or more of the time

2. Work environment involves everyday risks or discomforts that require normal safety precautions typical of such places as offices or meeting rooms, e.g., use of safe workplace practices with office equipment and avoidance of trips and falls

This job description is not intended as, nor should it be construed as, exhaustive of all responsibilities, skills, efforts, or working conditions associated with this job.

Reasonable accommodations may be made to enable individuals with disabilities to perform the essential functions of this job.

---

of the overall compensation project. If employees feel confident that the job descriptions are accurate and current, they will likely feel more confident about the quality of matches in salary data provided by other systems because these will have been based on the job descriptions. Even experienced consultants obtain agreement on the job description format up front, draft the descriptions from the data collected from employees, and submit the draft descriptions back to the client. Also allow time for one revision, if necessary.

FINAL APPROVAL

As the final authority for review and approval of all job descriptions, some library systems appoint a committee such as a board and human resources staff committee, a committee that includes a cross section of staff members, or a labor (if unionized) or staff association committee. Select the method that best fits your culture and politics for review, but ultimately designate one person for final approval (e.g., a senior human resources professional if the library system has one or the library director or assistant director in a smaller system). In addition, this person could be held accountable for updating the job descriptions periodically—however, all employees and supervisors should play a role in the process as well. The employee and supervisor should review job descriptions at least annually as a part of the performance management process.

Note

1. Peter Vaill, *Managing as a Performing Art: New Ideas for a World of Chaotic Change* (San Francisco: Jossey-Bass, 1989).

5

Context and Compensation Philosophy

After developing a commitment to your compensation plan, planning the compensation study, analyzing jobs, and writing job descriptions, you will want to think through some of the important issues regarding the library's compensation philosophy and pay policy. It is never a good idea to adopt another organization's compensation system because there really is no "one-size-fits-all" library plan. Each library system must think through a number of issues, starting with "What do you hope your pay plan will accomplish?" For example, an entirely different design recommendation would be made if the average tenure of your workforce were greater than fifteen years and your library were in a stable (internal and external) environment than if you were losing your top performers who were only averaging one to three years with the system.

Your consultant—or if you are not using a consultant, the project manager—should ask senior management important questions that may include those listed in the next section. In some cases members of the library's board of trustees or the personnel committee should be interviewed as well to ensure that you have their perspective as you begin your design work. Including them increases buy-in by the board, and they are usually more comfortable during a final presentation since they have made a connection with you or your consultant personally as well as with the topic and have had the opportunity to provide their perspective. Interviews with trustees can be face-to-face in person or in groups as an agenda item of a regularly scheduled (or special) personnel committee or board meeting.

INTERVIEW QUESTIONS FOR
SENIOR MANAGEMENT AND THE BOARD

The questions that follow are a compilation of questions that were asked in an early phase of work in two recent projects. Included are more questions than would normally be asked. They show how this time can be used productively to get additional data that may be important for the *context* of the design and outcome of the project. After each question is a justification of why the response to the question is important or what to look for to understand the library's compensation philosophy.

ISSUES AND CHALLENGES

1. *What are the key issues and challenges (both short- and long-term) facing the library at this time?*

It is important to know where the library is going. The future direction of the library may not be in writing and may only be in the heads of library leadership. However, if the system is going to go through a major transition, face budget increases or decreases by a public funding body, transition to a "Nordstrom's" model of customer service, or replace most circulation clerks with self-check-out machines (to name but a few possibilities), these will be important to know as you plan for a compensation system that is durable beyond six months. Similarly, it is important to know if the library is in a very stable situation, employs a core group of competent and qualified employees, and plans to, for the most part, maintain the status quo.

If your library faces many possible changes, it is likely that you will want to design a flexible plan that reflects the market and has wider, open salary ranges. That is, your library should consider pay for performance, and your job descriptions should be broad while building in opportunities for job growth and development. Libraries in a stable environment might want to design a plan that values internal equity and is less flexible. (See question 5, following.)

THE COMPENSATION PLAN

2. *What should the library's compensation plan accomplish?*

If you hear "maintain internal relationships" or "reward longevity or length of service," yours will be a very different plan than if the responses include "reward performance," "pay according to the market," or "retain high performing employees."

3. *How would you describe the current total compensation package (including pay, benefits, retirement, time off, etc.) at the library? How does it compare with that of other employers?*

In addition to assessing compensation, it may be important to conduct a survey to learn about the benefits provided in your market because your benefits package can be a very important motivator—or demotivator—for recruitment and retention. Benefits can be very expensive to the library, and employees rarely have a complete understanding of the value of their benefit plan in actual dollars paid by the system and how it compares with other local organizations. While this may begin to change, public, academic, and school libraries generally offer benefits that are worth more than the norm in their area—a fact neither known nor appreciated by most library employees. Nonetheless, even when the quality of benefits is outstanding, many employees still focus upon the cash compensation. "What is my salary?" and "How am I being paid compared to others in *X*?" are the questions generally asked. Applicants rarely consider the value of benefits. This is especially true of the generation X and younger candidates for employment. Benefits are more of a retention tool for long-term service and older employees because they are concerned about health insurance and take seriously their vesting in the library's retirement system.

4. *What factors should drive pay at the library system—market, skills, performance, education, contribution, length of service, or other concerns?*

The answers to this question will tell you and the members of your review committee what the library and management value and want to reward. The design of your compensation system will need to reflect and support these values. It is not difficult to correlate what management values to the compensation program design. For example:

If management wishes to pay in accordance with the market, the design will focus upon obtaining, via custom-made and published surveys, salary data of employees in your marketplace (as you define it, see question 5).

- If a high value is placed upon length of service, your design will include provisions to award long-term employees additional salary—perhaps in excess of market rates—as part of their base pay or as a bonus paid in a separate check.

- If your system values performance, your design will reflect open ranges rather than steps (where all employees, regardless of the level of performance, are entitled to the same step upon completion of a year of service).

COMPETITIVE MARKET

5. *When employees leave your library system, where do they go? From where are new employees hired? Are there any areas where recruitment or retention is a problem?*

The answers to these questions will help you understand your market and thus target the sectors of the economy and specific public and private organizations from which you will want to collect data.

- Employees in nonexempt positions, such as clerk, administrative assistant, financial assistant, and driver, usually leave for and are hired from all types of organizations, both from the private and the public sectors, in the local area.

- The market for nonlibrary-specific professional employees, such as director of marketing, chief financial officer, accountant, and human resources representative, is both local and regional—with a focus on local—and often includes nonprofits as well.

- Recruiting practices for professional librarian positions, especially department heads and directors, are often regional or national, depending upon your library's needs and the market.

It will be important to learn about jobs for which recruitment and retention are problems to

- see if there are any patterns that may or may not relate to compensation causing the situation

- ensure that these positions are thoroughly studied and sufficient data collected

- consider extending the market studied for these positions from, for example, local and public to regional and private

ASSESSMENT

6. *From your perspective, what is working and not working with the current pay plan? How should it be changed?*

Often management sees a problem with a common thread in a compensation plan. An example is that management realizes that 80 percent of the library's employees are at or approaching the maximum of their pay grade. This is a symptom that might be indicative of a number of things: It could be that employees, as a group, are long tenured and have been given step increases each year, thus placing them near the maximum of their pay grade and possibly over the market rate for the position. It could also indicate that the ranges for the jobs are too narrow from the minimum to the maximum of the pay grade and do not allow for sufficient growth unless the ranges are moved regularly to match the market.

A variety of root causes might be attributed to each problem. Before setting out to "fix" the problem, each needs to be analyzed for its cause. Once you understand the cause and suggest ways to rectify the problem, you will need to consider findings and alternatives for correction in light of

the library's compensation philosophy

what is financially feasible in the short term as well as over time

what is politically feasible in both the short and long term

7. *If there is a point factor system in place, from your perspective, what's working and not working with it? How, if at all, should it be changed?*

This question is asked when a library system uses a point factor system to evaluate jobs. (See the next chapter.) A typical problem with internally focused job evaluation plans is that if you were to assign a salary grade to "hot spot" jobs in a range that is reflective of the points received, you would not be able to fill those positions because market rates are generally higher than the point values. Therefore, to meet market demand, job evaluators ultimately make the points fit the market. Unless this is documented, it puts the plan out of whack.

8. *What is the appropriate balance between external market equity and internal job worth?*

Here you are attempting to see what should drive pay rates when the results of the market study are inconsistent with the point factor or other internal job evaluation results. This response will also guide your work even when designing a market-based pay plan. Since you will not be surveying all library jobs (see chapter 7), you will need to slot nonbenchmark jobs. Reviewing the internal value of the job in addition to what you know about the market will aid in this effort. (Note: Those of you who have experience with library compensation programs will be familiar with these concepts; other readers will learn about them in chapter 7.)

9. *Are there any issues of concern regarding the distribution of job responsibilities in your department?*

Because compensation is a component of your human resources system, a project often extends beyond the boundaries of a compensation project. The information you learn from this question is often helpful in job design and in activities seeking more alignment of roles with goals or an enhancement of efficiency and effectiveness. This is a question that may not be appropriate to ask—depending upon the scope of your project.

10. *For what positions is an MLS necessary? Why? What librarian functions are being performed? What are the essential functions of an MLS librarian in this library system?*

Motivated in part by the tight labor market for credentialed librarians as well as by financial limitations, some public libraries are looking at the roles of professional librarians—along with those inherent in other employee categories—to ensure that employees are performing the highest level duties in their classifications and that the lowest level work is pushed down to the lowest possible level. So, while we all compose letters on computers, administrative support personnel, rather than librarians or department heads, should send out the mailings.

In addition, a library that encourages employees to return to school for a bachelor degree or an MLS will have some different pay policies and practices from a system that only recruits applicants who already hold an MLS degree. Similarly, a system that wants to reward employee longevity will have a different pay plan from one that places a high premium on goal achievement. Finally, systems that are planning to downsize, reorganize to use MLS positions only at the management level, or open branches in many new communities will have different goals and consequently different pay plans. A library system that can't afford to hire any staff with an MLS degree will truly need to design creative pay plans *and* take the time to consider how it staffs and services its customers in the most effective way. Finally, if your library is talking about requesting that applicants for branch manager positions have an MBA or coursework in business, that, too would be important information to have.

ABILITY TO IMPLEMENT A COMPENSATION PROGRAM

11. *What is the financial position of the library system? What resources have been approved or funded to implement adjustments if necessary?*

It is important that funds have been, or can be, set aside to implement at least partial salary adjustments. It simply is not good for morale to conduct a compensation study and to leave it on a shelf. There should be a commitment to at least partial funding, in accordance with resources, and to implementation over time to the extent feasible.

12. *What should the library pay in relation to the market? At the market value? A little below? Above it?*

While most library systems say they would like to pay at the going market rate, some find that their financial position does not allow it or that their benefits are so outstanding they choose to pay *x* percent (usually 90 percent) of market rate. One library needed help designing a three-year implementation plan to achieve paying employees 90 percent of market. Needless to say, it was quite a bit behind the market.

Other library systems are willing to pay above-market rates to attract and retain the best-qualified employees. A recent public-sector client wanted a system flexible enough to generally pay at market but to go above the market rate for employees in "hot spot" jobs or for high performers.

COMMUNICATIONS

13. *What, if anything, do employees know about this project?*

As internal consultants to this project, you may not need the answer to this question; however, external consultants would like to know. Often the answer "Employees are fully aware of the study; it's been communicated in a variety of ways" is not consistent with reality when you begin conducting focus groups, interviews, or employee presentations. "What study?" the employees may say.

OTHER

14. *Are there any issues you should be aware of that may have an impact on this project?*

Again, as employees working within the system, you may not need to ask this question if you have a good idea about history and current events in the library's life. Consultants, on the other hand, ask this question because they

know that the compensation study is only one of many events. For example, employees may be jaded due to the results (or lack of results) from prior studies, and there might be but a limited amount of management and employee time to work on this project due to other priorities. If a new software system is about to be installed and all employees are to be trained in its use, or if all technical processing functions are going to be outsourced, it's important to know this early on in the process so that the work plan can account for it and answers to employee concerns and considerations can be prepared.

15. *What would be a successful outcome of this project for you? How can its success be ensured?*

External consultants always want to ensure that they are meeting the goals set by their clients. If you have been appointed project manager or a member of the review committee by senior management in your library system, you should discuss the criteria for success in advance of the project as well.

Do not limit your inquiry of success criteria to the opinions of senior management. Ask employees this question as well, attempting to gauge their expectations. When they run in extremes, i.e., "I expect a huuuuge salary increase because I don't earn nearly enough" or "Nothin's gonna happen anyway," you may be able to help them frame realistic goals and talk about management's commitment.

Framework for Posing Context Questions

The preceding were just sample questions. When you prepare for your interviews with management and the board, think through the purpose of each of your questions. Think about the following:

What do you need to know?

Why?

What information will the responses to this question give you?

What, if anything, can you do with this information?

At the end of the interview process, will you have all of the information you need to understand the compensation and related issues facing the library, to draft a compensation philosophy, and to select and propose the design components of the pay plan?

Thus, for each question, make sure its answer will provide you with information you need and can use. It is generally not a good idea to ask questions that are not at all relevant to your project. Sometimes it is even detrimental because those interviewed might think something may change when, indeed, nothing is planned.

After you complete the interviews, you might find it helpful to compile the data in a simple Power-Point presentation and review it with management and the review committee. Include a draft of the compensation philosophy with the presentation for discussion and to ensure that it captures the intent of management. The next section of this chapter will give you an overview of what a compensation philosophy is and how to craft one.

COMPENSATION PHILOSOPHY

A compensation philosophy is a clear statement of intent that is developed to guide compensation decisions made during the project and afterward. It should reflect a clear understanding of the library's intentions and desired level of competitiveness with the market. It should be published and serve as a reference for managers and employees on how the library will handle compensation decisions. In general, a compensation philosophy is a guiding statement. Its components include

- goals and objectives
- definition of your marketplace
- desired degree of competitiveness with your market

Examples of brief, actual compensation philosophies adopted by library systems follow.

EXAMPLE 1
Anytown Public Library

Anytown Public Library seeks to recruit and retain well-qualified, highly motivated employees and to compensate employees for their contribution to the library's mission and for meeting their goals and for innovation, risk-taking, and continuous improvement.

Guidelines

Jobs will be assigned to salary grades and ranges. Each range will be reflective of, and externally competitive with, the appropriate market for that job. The guideline for external competitiveness of salary ranges is the market median of the range minimum. Salary ranges will be revised and updated regularly to reflect the market.

Originally included in this compensation philosophy, and then excluded due to potential fiscal constraints, was the following:

Anytown Public Library provides tuition reimbursement and supports skills improvement and career development for employees.

This philosophy also indicates what Anytown Public Library values in its employees, and hence what it will reward: contribution, innovation, risk-taking, and continuous improvement.

EXAMPLE 2
ABC Public Library System

The goal of the ABC Public Library System's compensation plan is to recruit and retain qualified, competent employees to best serve the needs of a growing and diverse community.

ABC Public Library System's salary ranges balance competitiveness with the external market and with internal equity. In general, the comparable market consists of libraries and public jurisdictions in the region. The comparable market for "hot" (in-demand) professional and management jobs may include private industry in the region. Competitive is defined as the median salary and/or salary ranges of the market.

This philosophy indicates that both internal and external equity are valued and important to the library. It also differentiates "hot" jobs by broadening the definition of the labor market to include private sector organizations.

EXAMPLE 3
Public University

The goal of Public University's compensation plan is to establish and maintain a market-based salary program with salary ranges that are competitive with a broad mix of industries in the regional marketplace and with public doctoral institutions of similar size.

Jobs will be assigned to salary ranges based on the median value of similar jobs in the marketplace.

Within these salary ranges, employees will be paid for their individual performance and contribution to the campus mission.

This organization's philosophy clearly states that its is a market-based compensation plan. It defines its market broadly, informing the reader that private companies are part of its marketplace. It also clearly articulates a reward system based on performance.

EXAMPLE 4
XYZ Public Library

The goal of XYZ Public Library's compensation plan is to recruit and retain qualified employees. XYZ Public Library's salary ranges will be set at the market to achieve this objective.

The market for professional positions is public libraries in the region.

The market for nonexempt, nonlibrary positions is local.

Internal equity is very important.

XYZ Public Library encourages career development and lateral and upward mobility within the library system; it does not provide extra compensation for specialized skills (e.g., computer search skills or second language ability).

A compensation philosophy does not ordinarily respond to a single issue—such as the one for specialized skills in example 4. In this case, it was a controversial issue because some employees were paid for specialized skills while others were not. Implementation of the new pay plan was to have eliminated the need to consider extra compensation for specialized skills. Since it was contentious, it was decided to clarify it (and "lay it to rest" according to the human resources director) in the compensation philosophy.

EXAMPLE 5
A Maryland Public Library

The goal of QRS Public Library's compensation plan is to recruit, retain, and motivate highly qualified employees. Our salary ranges should achieve a balance of being competitive with the external market as well as internally equitable and should reflect the median salary offered by the market. The comparable market for professional library positions is Anne Arundel, Baltimore, Carroll, Frederick, Cecil, and Howard County public libraries. The comparable market for all other positions is a combination of library systems and other local public- and private-sector employers.

Salaries to new hires should be offered and increases awarded based on a combination of factors including related experience, education, licenses, etc.

Example 5 is taken from a public library in Maryland. This philosophy, a little different from the others, identifies the local county public libraries with whom they compete for professional librarian positions.

COMPENSATION POLICY DESIGN COMPONENTS

In addition to a brief philosophy statement, or as a substitute for it, a more-detailed policy can be created to delineate details of the compensation plan, including selected criteria and responsibilities of senior management and the board of trustees. An example of such a policy is shown in worksheet 7.

Begin to think about options and personalize a philosophy for your organization. To get started, fill in the blanks in worksheet 7 as follows:

a. Insert a brief goal statement or mission for your compensation philosophy. What do you want the compensation plan to accomplish? Think about recruitment, retention, internal/external equity, etc.

b. Identify how the compensation system will be developed. Will you use a consultant? Will you work internally to develop the plan?

c. Select/identify goals of the compensation system. Will you focus solely on external equity? If so, who constitutes your market? Will the market be the same for all positions? Will you use published data? Or will you include a mix of internal and external equity?

d. Identify who will be responsible for ensuring the ongoing administration and upkeep of the compensation program.

e. Identify who will be responsible for recommending changes and updates to salary ranges. Do you have an internal compensation team? Will the human resources director perform this function?

f. Identify who will have ultimate responsibility and accountability for ensuring the fairness, equity, and consistency of pay adjustments.

As you can see from the worksheet, you will need to gather important information before beginning to design the compensation plan. What you learn from senior management will provide you with the answers to the following:

1. Who is our *market?* That is, who are our competitors for human capital?

2. What is our level of *competitiveness?* Do we want to lead the market, match it, or set our rates behind it? Keep in mind that your choice will not only have an impact on your salary budget, it will also affect your library's culture. For example, an above-market pay policy can contribute to a feeling of selectiveness or elitism—in the very best sense of these words. Employees might feel that they are the best and are delighted to be members of the library system. A low pay level can contribute to the opposite culture, sometimes leading to below-par contributions and employees looking to leave. This impact, however, can be minimized given a mission-driven culture and management practices that value employees.

3. Are we going to base our pay plan on *individuals and their competencies* or *on the job?* This book assumes that *jobs* will be evaluated rather than the individuals performing them. In the event your library selects a method of compensation that is person-based, you will still need to collect market data to establish appropriate pay ranges.

When job-based pay is used, the assumption is that the worth of the job can be determined in the marketplace or via an internally focused job evaluation methodology and that employees (individually and as a group) performing the job are worth (only) as much to your library as the job itself is worth on the market. In chapter 10, a broad overview of skill- and knowledge-based pay is presented. In these types of systems, individuals are rewarded for increasing their skills or knowledge.

4. Will pay be based on *performance* or will a *step system,* one that provides for the same annual increase to all but the most unsatisfactory employees, be designed? An overview of performance-based pay is provided in chapter 9.

5. Is the focus on the compensation plan going to be *internal* or *external* equity? The intent of an internal equity–driven system is to ensure that employees performing similar work are paid similarly and jobs with similar value to the organization share the same pay ranges. Conversely, the goal of an external-equity focused system is to pay employees in accordance with the market. These concepts will be fully covered in chapters 7 and 8, where the tools are provided to design compensation plans based on these systems.

An advantage of an internally based system is that it can lead to or support a culture of homogeneity and a feeling of fair and equal treatment. On the other hand, because it may not attend to the salaries paid in the labor market, the library might have to pay more than necessary to attract and retain good employees just to maintain internal

A Compensation Policy

ABC PUBLIC LIBRARY'S COMPENSATION POLICY

The goal of *<library name>* is to *<a. Insert brief mission.>*

_____

_____

_____

_____

_____

_____

_____

_____

_____

_____

_____

For example: We believe that it is in the best interest of both the library system and our employees to fairly compensate our workforce for the value of the work provided. It is our intention to use a compensation system that will determine the current market value of a position based on the skills, knowledge, and behaviors required of a fully competent employee. The system used is objective and nondiscriminatory in theory, application, and practice. We have determined that this can best be accomplished by

<b. Select one of the following or draft one appropriate to your situation.>

☐ using a professional compensation consultant and system recommended by library management and approved by the board of trustees.

☐ using internal resources to develop a system approved by library management and submitted to the board of trustees.

Compensation System Goals

<c. Select all that apply.>

☐ 1. The compensation system will price positions to market by using appropriate local, regional, national, and library-specific custom-made and published survey data.

☐ 2. The market data will primarily include other library systems, local public jurisdictions *(if public library),* and not-for-profit organizations and will address significant market differences due to geographic location.

☐ 3. The system will evaluate external equity: market pricing of benchmark jobs compared with similar *<library name>* jobs.

(Continued)

☐ 4. The system will evaluate internal equity: the relative worth of each job when comparing the required level of job competencies, formal training and experience, responsibility, and accountability of one job to another and arranging all jobs in a formal salary grade structure.

<Select one.>

☐ Professional support and consultation will be available to design and implement a new market-pricing compensation system.

☐ The compensation team of *<library name>* will design and implement the compensation system. Professional resources, including books, local experts, and library or local government colleagues, will be made available to the team as necessary.

☐ 5. The compensation system must be flexible enough to ensure that *<library name>* is able to recruit and retain a highly qualified workforce while providing the structure necessary to effectively manage the overall compensation program.

☐ 6. The salary structure will be reviewed periodically to ensure market competitiveness.

☐ 7. The assistant director of finance and administration *<d. or select appropriate title>* is responsible for the ongoing administration of the program.

Library Board of Trustees Responsibilities

The board of trustees of *<library system name>* is responsible for the review of recommendations made by the library director and will give final approval for the new compensation system.

As part of the annual budgeting process the board of trustees will review and approve funds to be allocated for total compensation, which would include base salaries, bonuses or any other variable pay, and all other related expenses including benefit plans as recommended by management.

The board of trustees shall set the salary, salary range, and specific components of the total compensation package for the library director.

Management Responsibilities

The library director is responsible and accountable to the board of trustees. In that capacity the director is charged with ensuring that the library is staffed with highly qualified, fully competent employees and that all programs are administered within appropriate guidelines and within the approved budget.

On an annual basis the library director will review and approve recommended changes to the salary ranges as recommended by

<e. Select as appropriate.>

☐ the human resources director

☐ the compensation review team

☐ the assistant director of finance and administration

as determined through periodic market analysis.

The salary budget shall include an allocation for budget adjustments. However, the individual determinations for each employee's salary increase will be the responsibility of the library director. This includes such responsibilities as determining the appropriate staffing levels, titles, position levels, merit and promotional increases, and compensation consisting of salary and other discretionary pay for all positions.

The library director shall ensure that salary ranges are updated and individual jobs are market priced periodically and that pay equity adjustments are administered in a fair and equitable manner. The

<f. Select one.>

- ☐ deputy director
- ☐ director of human resources
- ☐ assistant director
- ☐ finance and administration
- ☐ other _____

is responsible to ensure that the total compensation program is managed for consistency and equity.

Signed _____

Date _____

---

relationships. Conversely, the library might not offer enough salary to attract candidates to fill "hot spot" jobs for which recruitment and retention are more difficult.

An important advantage of a compensation plan based on external equity is that it is sensitive to and competitive with the market. That is, pay rates and ranges are aligned with what is paid in the market. A disadvantage, however, is that implementing a compensation plan primarily focused on external equity can lead to the disruption of long-held relationships of positions to each other. An outgrowth of this change is possible feelings of lack of worth and inequity by those holding positions that may not be as highly valued as they were in an internally based system.

6. What role should *base pay* and *benefits* play in relation to total compensation? At the very least, you should have an idea of the value of your benefits plan and how it compares with the benefits of

your competitors. In addition, you should consider incentives and noncash awards as part of your compensation plan as well.

7. To what extent is *job security* essentially taken for granted? Unlike private companies, most library employees have not undergone major downsizing or restructuring. Where restructuring did occur, generally all employees were assured that they would not lose their jobs (although they might have been given different jobs in a different location).

8. Should the pay plan account for *contingent workers?* While many libraries use substitutes to augment their workforce, should plans be designed that consider a core and contingent workforce? Is that a possibility in your library system's future?

9. To what extent is your library system going to reward *seniority?* On the one hand, a job is only worth so much, but on the other, what is the message you want to send to employees—especially those with long service and those aspiring to long service?

6

Point Factor Job Evaluation System for Internal Equity

One of your goals is to create a compensation plan that is externally competitive, internally fair, and supportive of your library's compensation strategy. This chapter discusses internally focused job evaluation systems that support the library's values. The next chapter will provide the information you need to assess equity with the external labor market. Chapter 8 provides tools to help you design your compensation plan. Ultimately, jobs will be assigned to grades and pay ranges in your compensation plan based on job content and market value and/or internal equity, not on employee value or individual performance. While individual-based compensation systems are mentioned in chapter 10, this chapter and the next focus upon *job-based* pay. An exception relates to librarians in academic libraries eligible for faculty status. Job evaluation relating to these librarians will be discussed later in this chapter.

JOB EVALUATION

The underlying purpose of job evaluation is to create a job hierarchy, be it internally or externally focused, in which the relative position of each job (not job holder) within an organization can be easily identified. Job evaluation does not determine rates of pay—that comes later. The outcome of job evaluation is a job hierarchy that clearly depicts the relative importance of one job to another. It produces a ranking of jobs used by the library system in descending (or ascending) order, from the job that has the most accountability for setting and achieving strategic goals and objectives to one that is responsible for routine and clearly established tasks.

Even within a given industry such as library services, the relative order of jobs will change from institution to institution. For example, research skills and the knowledge of esoteric subject matter will likely be more valued in an academic or research library than in a branch of a local public library. In addition, the scope and responsibility of similar outreach efforts can range, for example, from involvement with local groups like the Kiwanis, community center, and Rotary Club to creating community partnerships, establishing literacy programs, developing senior and young adult programs, tracking homework assignments, and designing programs—all while directing the bookmobile to senior centers, day-care homes, and nursing homes. Thus, the same position in two different library systems will be used and valued differently and, subsequently, will be assigned to very different salary ranges based upon the scope of the job, level of responsibility, and contribution of the position to the library's mission.

Common Job Evaluation Plans for Measuring Internal Equity

The most commonly used job evaluation systems are whole-job ranking and point factor. Market pricing/ slotting is another method of job evaluation, but due to its external focus (in contrast to the internal focus of these plans) it will be discussed in greater detail in chapter 7.

Whole-job ranking is generally a more-subjective method than a point factor system. It seeks to make comparisons between whole jobs as opposed to breaking down jobs into their component parts. Point factor plans, on the other hand, break down and compare different parts or job components with each other.

Following are brief descriptions of these types of internally focused job evaluation systems. Included are brief descriptions of the pros and cons of each as well as of the externally focused method of job evaluation, market pricing. Figure 6.1 summarizes these advantages and disadvantages.

Whatever job evaluation system is selected, it should be flexible enough to adjust and adapt to changes within the library's world of work as well as the marketplace in general. The systems that appear to be the most useful are those that are

FIGURE 6.1   Comparison of Job Evaluation Methods

Method	Advantages	Disadvantages
Whole-Job Ranking	More flexible than point factor and other classification methods Less time-consuming than factor-based methods Supports trend toward broader class definitions Simplest method overall	Can become subjective and not as defensible Depending on the size of the library, can be as time-consuming as other methods Most effective for smaller units; judgment calls in larger units are open to inconsistencies While can show that one job is more important than another, there is no indication of how much more important (relative worth or value) Requires that job ranker be highly knowledgeable about all jobs
Point Factor Method	Defensible and objective measure of job worth Fairly easy to communicate and understand Supports internal equity when factors are applied consistently to all jobs Ensures accuracy, quality, and reliability	Does not easily adapt to market conditions, dual career ladders, or professional trends Time-consuming because of complexity and detail Can be too focused on "policing" (point counting) Factor and level definitions are often difficult to distinguish and may not apply to every classification or occupational group Maintenance and updates can be expensive
Market Pricing/ Slotting Method (Externally Focused)	Maintains market competitiveness More flexible than other methods Market data are available for most jobs	Can be time-consuming Slotting nonmarket-priced jobs can be subjective May reflect biases in the market (e.g., gender pay inequity)

efficient (i.e., do not require a large staff to maintain and allow for quick decision making)

based on a limited number of objective, predefined job characteristics

developed in conjunction with all key stakeholders (including managers, union representatives, and employees)

easily communicated to all employees

Whole-Job Ranking

Whole-job ranking is the simplest method of job evaluation. It involves looking at each job as a whole and positioning it in a hierarchy by ranking it against other jobs, using job descriptions, job titles, and the evaluators' knowledge of position duties and responsibilities. The result is a listing or ranking of jobs in order of relative importance. This method is limited in that it does not attend to the relative difference between positions—just that one is higher than the other. In addition, jobs are ranked without reference to any specific criteria. Sometimes ranking systems are as simple as gauging whether the job under study should be assigned a grade equal to, above, or below the position being rated.

Whole-job ranking can be seen as a subjective process. Raters shouldn't, but may be, influenced by current pay, the personality of the incumbent, or the perceived prestige of the job. It is also difficult to conduct whole-job ranking in complex, large library systems where there are many varied positions. Nonetheless, ranking can be a reliable job evaluation system, as those doing the ranking generally "know," with some degree of accuracy and reliability, which jobs are worth more than others in the library. Whole-job ranking, while not frequently used as the sole method of job evaluation, is often used instinctively as a check-in for reviewing the findings of point factor job evaluation.

Point Factor Plans

M. R. Lott created the point factor method of job evaluation in 1924. It is based on the analysis of jobs in terms of separately defined factors that are compensable to the library. That is, it employs the use of compensable factors, numerically scaled factor degrees, and weights reflecting the relative importance of each factor. Once the scaled degrees and weights are established for each factor, then each job is measured against each compensable factor, and a total score is calculated for each job. The total points assigned to a job determine the job's relative value and location in the pay structure. These points for each job can be arranged in a hierarchy from high to low or low to high, thus depicting the relative value of all library positions.

Point factor systems based on compensable factors are the most widely used internally focused job evaluation systems. While they can be complex because of the time and effort necessary for development and application, existing point factor systems can be purchased and adapted to your specific needs and values. Point factor plans offer a rationale for the differences in the ranking of jobs, provide documentation, and are objective. It is the recommended system for clients who want a more defensible internal equity system for evaluating each job than that provided by whole-job ranking. Keep in mind that since a point factor job evaluation system alone will not provide you with enough information to set salary ranges, it is advisable to obtain market data for at least 30 percent of your total jobs. In this manner you will have market rates to update or design your salary ranges, and then the ability to slot jobs into the market-based ranges following the application of the point factor plan.

Market Pricing

For maximum flexibility, using market pricing to ensure market-competitive pay rates is the typical recommendation. However, internal equity can be very important. When this is the case, a combination of a point factor system and market pricing is recommended. Market pricing is discussed in detail in the next chapter.

DESIGNING AND APPLYING A POINT FACTOR SYSTEM

Because it is the most widely used method of job evaluation for internal equity, the remainder of this chapter will take you through the process of designing your own customized point factor plan. It will then outline the steps you will need to follow to evaluate your jobs for internal equity. The following steps would be used whether you custom design or adapt an existing plan:

> charter and train a job evaluation committee
>
> select compensable factors
>
> select factor weights
>
> identify degrees in each factor
>
> apply the point factor system (evaluate jobs)
>
> review final rankings
>
> present findings

STEP 1
Charter and Train a
Job Evaluation Committee

Whether you choose to design your own point factor system or purchase and modify an existing one, you should go through the process with a committee. Invite no more than five to seven people, a subgroup of the review committee, to serve on a job evaluation team. If additional information is needed to evaluate a specific job, the incumbent or a supervisor of the position can be interviewed separately or invited to attend a portion of one of the meetings.

The art of job evaluation is to reconcile varied and legitimate views of the same position. Of course, you can't expect the committee to know how to evaluate jobs at the outset of the project. You must train the committee first and allow for practice before beginning this process. You can easily design a training and practice from the information provided in this chapter.

Convene a committee to review the factors and weights and, eventually, to evaluate the jobs themselves. These individuals should include employees who are knowledgeable about the library system and respected by other employees. Employees tend to trust the process—and results—much more readily when they know that their peers and colleagues were involved throughout the study instead of management conducting the entire project behind closed doors or "in secret."

STEP 2
Select Compensable Factors

Start with the articulation and definition of compensable factors. A compensable factor is any job attribute that provides the basis for determining the worth of a job. Most generic compensable factors include required skill and effort, responsibility, and working conditions. Within each factor there are other aspects of job content, for example, experience, knowledge, and required licenses might be found within the "skill" factor.

It is helpful to get buy-in from management and the review committee when identifying, defining, and weighing compensable factors. The factors need to reflect your library system's values and direction and enable you to differentiate levels of responsibility within the library. Many libraries have chosen point factor plans as their job evaluation method. No two have ever identified the exact same set of factors, nor have any two ever assigned the same weights to the factors once the factors have been selected. Most use some or all of the following factors and subfactors:

- education/training
- experience
- customer relations/service
- communications/key interactions
- supervision
    level of supervisory responsibility
    number of employees supervised
    level of supervision received
- job complexity
- problem solving
- decision making
    authority
    impact
- working conditions
    physical effort
    environmental factors

A streamlined job evaluation system includes the following factors:

- education and experience

- complexity
- impact
- customer relations
- working conditions

Once factors are identified, a clear definition of each must be written. Measure results and observable outcomes rather than tasks or subjective opinions. State ideas clearly and as concisely as possible; be specific. Write the factors so as to encourage evaluators (and employees, as they will see these factors in the job analysis questionnaire) to think about the *position,* not the person. Even including such simple statements as "the *job* requires *X*" can help keep the focus on position requirements in contrast to individual attributes and performance.

Determining which factors are important to your library system is a good exercise for the review committee. It fosters good dialogue about what factors are really important to the library and should be used as measures of relative job worth. Aim to include only one issue or consideration per factor. That is, limit your definition of each factor to as few measurement dimensions as possible. For example, do not include problem solving and decision making or scope and effect in the same factor definition. Doing so makes it more difficult to find the appropriate "fit" for each position. Describe issues only once, that is, in only one factor. Do not evaluate the same issue in more than one factor. For example, if customer service is a factor, don't measure it again in the problem-solving factor.

STEP 3
Select Factor Weights

Assigning factor weights is neither as difficult nor as daunting a task as it might sound. Follow these steps:

a. Involve the review committee. It encourages some real thinking about not only what factors are important but about *how* important they are. If customer service is a high priority in your mission and values statements, it should be weighted more heavily than, for example, supervisory responsibility.

b. Take into account the nature of the work performed by all of the positions that will be covered under the job evaluation plan. The positions generally range from the entry-level position of delivery driver to the experienced, professional positions such as manager.
c. Rank in order of importance the factors selected.
d. Determine the initial weights of each factor as a percentage of 100.

It may help to create a worksheet similar to worksheet 8. This worksheet lists the factors and leaves space for the ranking and percentage of weight that should be assigned to each. An example is provided in the worksheet that includes working conditions as bonus points to be added to the total points accumulated for the other factors. You may also choose to address these factors this way, depending on their level of importance to the library.

Ask each member of the team and management to complete the worksheet individually. Gather the individual responses, and use a flip chart to share them if you are working with a group. Going around the room, factor by factor, list everyone's answers. Mean, median, and mode of responses are easy to spot.

With the assistance of a facilitator, the group can then discuss each factor and work to reach consensus. You can start to move toward consensus by reviewing each factor one at a time and asking the person who gave the factor the lowest and the person who gave it the highest percentage of weight to talk about their rationale. Generally, most people respond within 5 to 10 percent of each other on each factor, and reaching consensus is not difficult because the people in the room are very familiar with the library and its values.

STEP 4
Identify Degrees in Each Factor

Next, break down each factor into levels or degrees. Following is an example pertaining to experience:

Factor group	Skill
Factor name	Experience

Factor Weights

Please rate the importance of each factor to meeting the mission, goals, and objectives of the library. Then, assign a weight of importance for each factor by allocating from 1 to 100 percent to each so that the total of the weights assigned to each of the factors is 100%.

Factor	% Weight Example	% Weight Your Library
1. Education/training	10	_____
2. Experience	10	_____
3. Customer relations	25	_____
4. Supervisory responsibility	10	_____
5. Number of employees supervised	5	_____
6. Level of supervision received	20	_____
7. Complexity	20	_____
8. Decision-making authority	0	_____
9. Decision-making impact	0	_____
Total		**100%**

Working Conditions	Bonus Points Example	Bonus Points Your Library
Physical effort	10	_____
Environmental factors	5	_____

Factor description This factor measures the amount of previous experience normally required to achieve satisfactory performance in the position.

Degrees
1. less than 6 months
2. 6 months to 1 year
3. 1 to 3 years
4. 3 to 5 years

This suggests that when evaluating positions you should look at how much experience is required of the incumbent prior to taking the job with the library. For example, you might hire a circulation or library assistant with little or no relevant experience, and therefore the position would be assigned degree 1. On the other hand, the experience requirement for the director of outreach position might be 4 to 5 or more years. Thus, the position would be assigned degree 4.

Your next step is to create a draft of the highest and lowest degrees in each factor. For example, if it is determined that a Ph.D. would not be a minimum qualification for even the highest level job in the library, then Ph.D. would not be included as a degree within the education factor. Similarly, if incumbents in all positions were required to hold an associate of arts or sciences degree as a minimum requirement, this would then serve as the lowest level (degree) indicated for the education factor, rather than the standard "ability to read and write."

When the highest and lowest degrees in each factor are defined, it is then necessary to determine the number of intermediate degrees needed. For example, if the system has "ability to read and write" as the lowest degree in the education factor and "master's degree in library sciences" as the highest degree, the final scheme for degrees of the education factor might be

1. Ability to read and write
2. Completion of high school or general equivalency diploma
3. Completion of associate of arts or associate of sciences degree
4. Completion of bachelor of arts or bachelor of sciences degree
5. Completion of master's degree in library sciences, information technology, or relevant field

Note: If you are determining degrees for an academic or special library, you may require another degree (number 6) if additional training is a requirement, for example, biology in a medical library or a law degree in a law library.

The appropriate degree in each factor would then be assigned to each position based upon *what is needed* to successfully perform the job. The individual employee's level of experience, education, or performance is *not* taken into consideration when assigning degrees to each position. In addition, it is important to remember that you must consider the job in its present state, not what would be *nice* to have.

When defining degrees of compensable factors, be aware that having too *many* degrees can result in having to

force artificial distinctions between degrees

require very detailed job analysis questionnaires or other forms of job documentation

increase the amount of time necessary to evaluate jobs

justify job reclassification denials

The latter point refers to an employee or manager attempting to obtain a job upgrade based on a poorly defined distinction between degrees in one or more categories. That is, employees often seek to have a degree moved higher on any factor hoping that it will raise the grade levels to which their jobs are assigned.

Conversely, having too *few* degrees can present a problem as well. You may experience difficulty assigning a degree if there's too large a progression from one level to the next, and the number of degrees you have may not fully cover all of the work performed.

Although you should try to have only one issue per factor, you may not always achieve that aim. For instance, you may find that, in the interest of streamlining your point factor system, it may be practical to combine factors, for example, *complexity* and *problem solving* as one factor. This one factor identifies the extent to which the job must use analytical and problem-solving skills in performing varied activities as well as the amount of independent judgment used by the incumbent. The benefit of such a factor is that you are gathering more in-depth information about each job. However, one drawback to factors such as these is that it may become increasingly difficult to identify *one* specific factor that best fits each job. Therefore, you may find that it is helpful to break factors down into component parts. For instance, if you are attempting to identify decision-making skills, you could refer to *decision-making authority* (the independence an incumbent may use in making decisions without referring to a supervisor) as well as *decision-making impact* (the potential outcome and effect of the types of decisions made by the incumbent). That is, will the decisions generally affect individuals or their immediate work areas, or is the impact of decisions organizationwide?

If a factor includes more than one issue, describe them in *each* degree. That is, if a given issue is in one degree, it needs to be described in each degree within the factor. For instance, a combined factor may include the issues of *complexity* and *problem solving*. In the following example, each of the four factors addresses both job complexity and the problem-solving skills required.

1. Work duties are well-defined with clear instructions or standard routines. Work is highly

structured, and independent judgment may be used in routine matters such as changing the order in which tasks are completed. Guidance is readily available.

2. Work regularly involves making choices about how to address problems in the work situation. Work involves moderately complicated procedures and tasks requiring independent judgment to select options or interpret data.

3. Work is complex and varied. It requires selection and application of technical or detailed skills to develop new solutions in a variety of work situations. A considerable degree of independent judgment is required to vary from established procedures and to develop methods for accomplishing work objectives.

4. Work is extremely complex and varied and requires a complete knowledge of a wide variety of operations, practices, and disciplines. Work consistently involves dealing with situations, facts, and problems that have not been previously addressed. Work consistently involves a considerable degree of independent judgment to develop and implement ideas.

STEP 5
Evaluate Jobs

Depending on the number of positions in your system and the available time of committee members, you may not be able to evaluate all positions in committee. It is best to evaluate at least half your total positions as a group, although the more the better. Your project manager, human resources staff, or a smaller evaluation team can evaluate the remaining positions.

When developing a list of positions to evaluate with the group, try to select positions that cover a large percentage of library staff. For instance, evaluating library associate, department head, librarian, and circulation assistant will most likely cover many staff members. In addition, try to select positions that encompass all levels of responsibility within the library. In other words, don't evaluate only the management or professional positions and skip over lower-level or entry-level positions. Following both of these hints will ensure that your job

evaluation process is fair and equitable and covers the largest percentage of library staff possible. For example, a large urban library system with a central or main location as well as twelve city and suburban branches evaluated the following positions:

Main Library	*Branch*	*Other*
page	page	terminal
page/clerk	clerical technician	operator
clerk I	clerk I	data editor
clerk II	clerk II	stock
clerk III	clerk III	handler
clerical supervisor	clerical supervisor	
clerical technician	library assistant	
library assistant	staff librarian	
staff librarian	senior staff librarian	
senior staff librarian	department head	
unit head	division head	
assistant department head		
department head		

A small library with two branches in a rural/resort area evaluated the following:

manager, adult services
manager, automated systems
manager, youth services
electronic outreach librarian
circulation manager
jail librarian
building maintenance/services manager
manager, technical services
bookmobile manager
cataloger
library associate
technical assistant—automation
accountant/bookkeeper
library aide—bookmobile
janitor/security
library aide/bookkeeper
library aide—circulation (full-time)
ILL assistant (part-time)
senior administrative specialist
library aide—circulation (part-time)
library aide—technical services
library aide—mending (part-time)
page

To help the committee focus upon the evaluation process and on each of the jobs to be evaluated, ask different committee members to review some of the JAQs and make a brief (two- to three-minute) presentation summarizing the job and its salient features. Ask the presenter to describe the jobs in a job family, for example, senior branch manager, branch manager, and assistant branch manager. By doing so, the committee can easily see the distinctions in a hierarchy within a job family.

Select Degrees

This method of job evaluation basically involves applying the point factor system to the library's jobs. That is, first indvidually and then collectively, the members of the committee will, job by job, select the degree in each factor that most closely describes but does not exceed the job being evaluated.

When members of the committee disagree, the group should work toward consensus. Consensus does not necessarily mean that everyone is in full agreement. Rather, it means that each member of the committee believes that he or she has had the opportunity to be heard, can "live with" the decision, and does not choose to block consensus. Anyone can block consensus. When this happens, suggest that the committee move on to the next position and revisit the unresolved position(s) at another time. The converse is also true because job evaluation is sometimes a subjective and human process. That is, instead of blocking consensus, sometimes group members "go along" with the majority when they shouldn't.

After discussion, apply the point factor plan to jobs within job families. You may use worksheet 9 to structure this process. That is, write the name of a job in the left-hand column. For example, you might start with library assistant I, II, and III.

Then select the appropriate degree for each factor and for each job. The degree for education/training for the library assistant I might be "1" (high school education or equivalent) and "1" may be selected as well for the education/training factor for library assistant II because no additional education may be required for incumbents in or applicants for this level of library assistant. The educational

requirement for library assistant III might increase to a degree of "2" if post-high school education or an associate degree is the minimum requirement for entry into this position. The evaluation, or application of the point factor plan, for the library assistant positions would continue as degrees were reviewed and selected for the remaining factors—experience, customer relations, etc. After degrees for each factor have been assigned to the positions in the library assistant job family, continue in a similar manner with another job family. Remember, now you are only selecting the *degree* for each factor.

During the job evaluation process, you may find that one or more factors for certain positions generate a great deal of discussion. If you can reach consensus only reluctantly, it is a good idea to make note of the discussion and its outcome. A "justification" worksheet (worksheet 10) is a good way to document the process in case the position needs to be revisited later. It also provides a way of ensuring that all parties have their opinions heard and noted. It can be used as backup documentation to explain or justify why you selected the degree you did in each factor. Alternatively, you can limit its use to those degrees that were controversial selections or to those instances when the decision to select one of two degrees was a difficult one.

Assign Points to Factors and Their Degrees

Having identified compensable factors and defined the degrees associated with each, you now have sufficient information to assign points to each degree. For ease of understanding, in the following examples it is assumed that each degree is of equal value in its distance to the next.

In determining points, the number of points of the first degree (degree 1) is the same as the factor weight or value (that is, the percentage of the total 100 percent allocated to it in worksheet 8). For example, if education is weighted at 20 percent, degree 1, "ability to read and write," would be 20. You can determine the top degree by multiplying degree 1 (with 20 points) by a multiplier of 10. Thus, the last degree, "completion of an MLS degree,"

Job Evaluation Rating by Position, Factor, and Degree

Job Title	Education/ training	Experience	Customer relations	Supervisory responsibility	Number of employees supervised	Level of supervision received	Complexity	Decision-making authority	Decision-making impact	Physical effort	Environmental factors	Total

Job Documentation Justification

Position: _____   Department/Location: _____

Date: _____

Factor	Degree	Justification
1. Education/training		
2. Experience		
3. Customer relations		
4. Supervisory responsibility		
5. Number of employees supervised		
6. Level of supervision received		
7. Complexity		
8. Decision-making authority		
9. Decision-making impact		
10. Physical effort		
11. Environmental factors		

would be 200. With a factor of 20 percent, the first and last degrees for education would be

Education Factor

Degree	Point Value
1	20
2	
3	
4	
5	200

Next, to find the value of the degrees between degrees 1 and 5, subtract the value of the first degree from the last degree:

$$200 - 20 = 180$$

Then, divide the difference (180) by 1 less than the number of degrees:

$$5 \text{ (degrees)} - 1 = 4$$
$$180 / 4 = 45$$

Since the result was 45, add 45 points to each degree, starting with the second as follows:

Education Factor

Degree	Point Value
1	20
2 (20 + 45)	65
3 (65 + 45)	110
4 (110 + 45)	155
5 (155 + 45)	200

For another example, assume that the factor "experience" is assigned a factor weight of 10 percent. There are 4 degrees from which the committee can select to evaluate the experience required:

Experience Factor
Degree

1. less than 6 months
2. two months to one year
3. one to three years
4. three to five years

Following the same principles established for the education factor, degree 1 would be allocated 10 points (the same as the factor weight) and the final degree, 4, would be assigned 100 points (10 times 10). Subtracting 10 from 100, 90 points remain. Dividing 90 by 3 (1 less than the number of degrees), tells us that 30 points would differentiate one degree from another, assuming equal value between degrees. The degrees allocated to experience would then be as follows:

Experience Factor

Degree	Point Value
1	10
2	40
3	70
4	100

Repeat the process for all other factors, ultimately creating a chart that might look something like this:

	Degree				
Factor	*1*	*2*	*3*	*4*	*5*
Education	20	65	110	155	200
Experience	10	40	70	100	
Complexity	etc.				

For the final summary, design a spreadsheet that looks very similar to worksheet 9 used by the committee. An example of a completed hierarchical ranking is shown in figure 6.2. The points associated with factor and degree weights have been entered into the spreadsheet. By position, enter the points for each degree in each factor. The result is a ranking of the library's positions by total points from the one with the most to the one with the least number of points.

STEP 6
Order and Review Final Rankings

Keep the session to a few hours and reconvene, if necessary. Build in time for review and validation of findings before final approval. Often jobs look very different when rank ordered than they do while evaluating them one at a time.

After a few days' sabbatical, committee members will bring a fresh perspective that is usually helpful. Generally speaking, it's best to start the review

FIGURE 6.2 Sample Hierarchical Ranking with Points

ANYTOWN PUBLIC LIBRARY
JOB EVALUATION RESULTS

Job Title	Education/ training	Experience	Customer relations	Supervisory responsibility	Number of employees supervised	Level of supervision received	Complexity	Decision-making authority	Decision-making impact	Physical effort	Environmental factors	Total
Central library manager	350	230	250	240	192	192	288	264	212	0	0	2,218
Adult coordinator	350	173	312	192	155	192	230	212	212	0	0	2,028
Facilities manager	200	230	250	192	115	192	288	212	212	0	0	1,891
Children's coordinator	350	173	312	144	38	192	230	212	212	0	0	1,863
Personnel manager	300	230	312	96	38	192	288	159	212	0	0	1,827
Assistant facilities manager	200	230	188	144	38	144	230	159	212	120	120	1,785
Trust and public relations manager	300	230	312	144	38	144	230	159	212	0	0	1,769
Senior branch librarian	350	173	250	144	155	144	173	159	159	0	0	1,707
Juvenile coordinator	350	173	312	0	0	192	230	212	212	0	0	1,681
Department heads	350	173	250	144	115	144	173	159	159	0	0	1,667
Branch librarian	350	173	250	144	76	144	173	159	159	0	0	1,628
Supervisor of circulation	250	173	250	144	115	144	173	159	159	0	0	1,567
First-class engineer	200	230	125	0	0	144	230	159	212	120	120	1,540
Assistant branch librarian	350	116	250	144	38	144	173	159	159	0	0	1,533
Outreach department manager	350	116	188	144	76	144	173	159	159	0	0	1,509
Children's department manager	350	116	188	144	38	144	173	159	159	0	0	1,471
Network and microcomputer administrator	300	173	188	96	38	96	230	159	159	0	0	1,439

meeting first thing in the morning—before employees get involved in daily operational issues or need to tackle the daily crisis. You can list all jobs by

total points

factor and degree (that is, all jobs that received a degree of *1* in the factor of education; all jobs that received a degree of *2* in education, etc.)

department total points, for example, in a public library environment, this will usually translate into

• branch jobs

- main library jobs
- finance and administration jobs
- maintenance and delivery; bookmobile drivers
- job family (e.g., circulation staff, librarian)
- management

Ask the committee to individually review the hierarchy to see if it makes sense. They should consider the following:

> Having gone through this process and given your knowledge of the library and its jobs, are you comfortable that each job contributing at the same or similar level is ranked with a similar point total?
>
> Do any jobs stick out like a "sore thumb" (and therefore not belong where they were slotted)?

This more or less brings the committee and other people reviewing its work to use the job ranking approach to job evaluation for validation. From experience, many of the information systems jobs are "sore thumbed" because very often the market requires their slotting into a higher grade in the library's structure than it would if decisions were made based upon point totals alone.

Once each committee member has had an opportunity to reflect on the results and make notes on inconsistencies found, it's time to return to the entire committee for final discussion and review. These two steps—individual and then group review—are important to validate the final results and should not be overlooked.

Experience has shown that there will be some jobs that are clearly ranked inappropriately. It happens in all committees. Therefore, talk it through together and review the degrees again. Some degrees may have been erroneously assigned, and that's ok. Now is the time to make any necessary changes.

After committee review, the project manager should review the final list with department heads. Depending on the culture of your library, share all or partial (their own organizational unit) findings with department heads, either individually or as a group. If a department manager uncovers a prob-

lem, review it for validity and determine whether to present it again to the review committee. Oftentimes, it's a misperception of the job or something that can be easily resolved during the meeting. Other times, it's a legitimate problem that will need to be addressed by the committee. Regardless of the outcome, don't forget to follow up with the department head. Other than just making good common sense, this also helps to build commitment to the process and buy-in.

STEP 7
Present Findings

After all the changes are made to the hierarchy and the differences are reconciled, it's time to present the plan to senior management, the library director, and others for their review and feedback. While some project teams might seek final approval at this point, it is best to wait until you have the results of your market pricing. (See chapter 7.) The reasons for this are that market findings might influence some assignments and rankings and senior managers are often hesitant to approve anything before having all the data—especially market information on difficult-to-recruit or other "hot skills" positions. However, at this point, do not change rankings again. Although the market rates may put positions in a higher or lower ranking, wait until you have all of the data, and highlight jobs that have inconsistent job evaluation and market findings for conversation and pay-policy considerations.

LIBRARIANS WITH FACULTY STATUS

For professional librarians in academic libraries who hold faculty status, the job evaluation exercise will not be relevant. Where librarian salaries are tied to faculty salaries, you will not need to market price their salaries either. An academic department or the college's human resources department will do that for you.

Generally, although not always, when librarians in academic settings hold faculty status, it is a nontenure appointment. Sometimes, although they are not eligible for tenure, librarians are eligible for "permanent" status after a defined number of years of service. In a system where all other exempt professional and administrative employees are termed "at-will" or "regular" at best, this is a benefit and a compromise position for not being on a tenure track.

In these institutions, as with faculty positions, there are defined qualifications for librarian rank, typically librarian I to librarian IV. The level I is reserved for an entry-level master's-prepared librarian. Movement to level II is typically based upon performance, continuing education, and experience and is more-or-less automatic for quality, high-performing librarians. Many librarians remain at this level because the requirements for advancement to the rank of librarian III are substantial. For example, one university library requires the following:

> Evidence of leadership, resourcefulness, innovation, and dedication. . . . Professional participation . . . should include refereed publications, papers presented at professional meetings, committee appointments, and holding office in professional organizations or similar activities that contribute to the advancement of the library profession or to an academic discipline related to the individual's position. Service at this rank should be characterized by leadership or significant participation of high quality.

The same library adds the following requirements for advancement to librarian IV:

> The Librarian IV must also demonstrate significant achievements in at least two areas of professional activity. Significant achievement in professional organizations at this rank can be demonstrated by activities such as holding a major office, serving as a committee chair, engaging in extensive committee work, or similar activities that contribute to the vitality of the library profession or to an academic discipline related to the individual's position. The involvement, effort, and contribution must be at a level that is recognized by others in the field.
>
> At this rank academic research and publication activities will be judged both by quality and extensiveness of activities. These activities should go beyond the occasional and reflect expertise recognizable by others in the field.

Promotions, as you can see, are based on professional activity as well as job performance—very different from the typical criteria or compensable factors in a public library. However, these requirements *clearly convey the values* of this academic library. This type of policy not only communicates the library's values but also is clear about what it will evaluate and reward.

7
Market Pricing

While chapter 6 detailed an internally focused job evaluation system and its application, this one looks outward. It presents an overview of how to collect external salary data and market price positions and reviews which jobs should be the focus of a custom survey, which libraries and other organizations should be surveyed, and why. A sample spreadsheet you can use to analyze data is included.

Libraries and other organizations use market pricing to establish pay structures and rates that are market sensitive. That is, they see what employees in comparable positions are paid. They also track movement of market rates to adjust or revise their pay structures. This provides a rational, objective basis for setting pay rates. Market pricing uses the labor market, adjusted by your compensation philosophy, to set rates at, above, or below the going market rate.

Whether or not you have created an internal ranking of library positions based on their value to your system, as outlined in chapter 6, you will still need to collect salary data for many of the library's jobs. During the market-pricing phase of this project you will gather information regarding the rates paid to employees holding similar positions in your market.

This chapter reviews how you can design, conduct, and analyze custom surveys to learn of your competitors' pay rates. You should consider developing two surveys. One will be sent to the libraries in your labor market as you have defined it. These libraries, be they public, academic, or special, will have positions that are similar to those of your library. The libraries you survey will be familiar with your terms for library positions and can easily determine the extent to which their jobs match yours. However, that is not the case with the second survey, which will be sent to organizations, local government jurisdictions, colleges, school boards, and nonprofit or for-profit organizations in your local labor market. Therefore, a more generic survey should be sent to those identified participants. The basic steps of market pricing are to

> establish your time line for this part of the project
>
> select benchmark positions to survey

target survey participants

decide if you will ask any questions about pay practices and benefits

design the questionnaire

use other market data sources if available

follow up with participants and verify responses

analyze and, if necessary, adjust data

prepare and send reports to participants

While these steps don't always happen in exactly this order, and they may be iterative, what follows is a "walk through" of each step of the process.

STEP 1
ESTABLISH A TIME LINE

Ascertain when you absolutely must have the cost of your new compensation plan finalized for budget submissions. Once you are ready to assess the fiscal impact of your new compensation plan, you will essentially be finished with the project. From the date of your presentation for approval by the board of trustees, local governing body, or academic administrators, work backward to determine your starting date. Depending on the timing of your survey, and in consideration of other activities that may be occupying staff time (end of fiscal year activities, technology installation, technical processing study, or salary planning), as well as the length of your survey and whom you are surveying, you should plan at least eight to twelve weeks to develop and send out the survey, compile and tabulate findings, and analyze results. When planning your time line, don't forget that you will need to develop the salary structure and implementation plan (see chapter 8) and obtain approvals as well.

Generally you can schedule survey activities parallel with other tasks (e.g., creating and applying a point factor job evaluation plan) and begin this step very, very early in the project. (See the appendix for a complete project time line.) For example, if you plan to cost out your new pay plan and implement it on July 1, depending upon your approval process, the survey should be ready to be mailed no later than January 1. Larger, more-complex systems and academic libraries generally require more

time for completion of market pricing than do smaller ones.

The survey process is very time-consuming and, generally speaking, will always take longer than you plan, so build in plenty of time. Determine how much time you will need to draft the survey and have it reviewed by the committee and any other individuals involved in the approval process. Keep in mind that there will be suggestions for revisions, especially regarding the benchmark jobs selected and summary position descriptions. Make sure you plan time to follow up with participants after receiving their responses. Of two things you can be certain: There *will* be questions, and you *will* need to verify the data once it is received. Develop a detailed work plan and stick to it.

STEP 2
SELECT BENCHMARK POSITIONS TO SURVEY

Select the positions in the library's structure that will serve as benchmark jobs to be included in the survey sent to other organizations. Benchmark positions are easily understood, are used by other libraries or area employers, and should represent all levels and types of work performed throughout the library structure. It is important to include jobs that have many incumbents, although you will also include several single-incumbent positions such as department heads, assistant directors, and the library director. In selecting benchmark jobs, consider these guidelines. Surveyed jobs should be

easy to describe

varied in terms of required education and experience

used by other employers

representative of all levels of the library

stable and not in the process of changing (so that matches are comparable)

representative of a large percentage of the employee population

jobs for which you are having trouble recruiting and retaining (i.e., "hot skills" jobs, department heads, MLS librarians)

Since you will be sending out a survey to nonlibrary participants, select jobs those participants will be interested in, for example, an entry-level clerk, accountant, office manager, systems administrator, network manager, and facilities manager.

While you might like to survey all of your library's benchmark jobs, please don't (unless your system is very small and including all jobs does not result in a survey of overwhelming length). As you draft the survey instrument, consider the reader of or responder to your survey—the one who will ultimately decide whether to complete it. Respondents may be overwhelmed if you ask for information regarding too many positions or ask too many questions.

Include the most important benchmark jobs—those most important to your library and those that encompass the majority of your employable population, such as librarian (BLS and MLS), library associate, circulation clerk, and so forth—and cover the system both vertically and horizontally. An example of the jobs surveyed for a large urban library follows.

library director	library associate
assistant library director	automation/technology
manager of central	manager
library	computer operations
central library	manager
department manager	PC network manager
managing librarian, branch	workstation support
services	technician
subject specialist	computer training
reference librarian	specialist
branch librarian	accountant
(various levels)	shelver
collection development	circulation supervisor
coordinator	circulation clerk
children's services	personnel manager
coordinator	supervising cataloger
public relations	library technician
manager	children's specialist
development manager	(BS/MLS)
buildings manager	

In this same large system a local survey went out to community colleges, public school systems, banks, county governments, and other private-sector nonlibrary organizations. The following were benchmarked jobs for that local survey:

reference librarian	administrative
buildings manager	assistant
PC network manager	secretary
workstation support	teacher (BS and MS)
technician	security guard
accountant	purchasing agent
office clerk	personnel manager
data entry clerk	

A small regional library benchmarked the following jobs to survey:

library administrator	automation technician
information services	library assistant (ILL)
librarian	administrative
librarian	assistant
catalog librarian	library assistant
manager, automation	(administrative)
services	delivery driver

How many jobs should you survey? If market pricing is your only method to evaluate jobs and create a salary structure, you should collect data for at least 50 percent of your jobs. If the market data is augmenting a point factor or other job evaluation plan, obtaining market data for 25 to 30 percent of the jobs will suffice.

Using information gathered during job analysis is critical for ensuring that jobs are matched properly to jobs in other organizations. You will need to draft an up-to-date summary for each job included in the survey to facilitate the respondents' ability to accurately determine if they have an appropriate match. Examples of two such summaries follow.

Cataloging manager: Responsible for cataloging materials and for bibliographic database management; creates original cataloging as necessary; develops and maintains authority files; supervises two full-time cataloging assistants; requires master in library science and two years' library or cataloging experience

Acquisitions supervisor: Supervises acquisitions operations and staff; orders materials in a timely fashion from the most cost-efficient source; responsible for understanding, setup, and maintenance of the Data Research Associates acquisitions program used for ordering, receiving, and serials check-ins; establishes or revises acquisitions procedures; requires associate of arts degree *or* two years of job-related experience beyond high school

STEP 3
TARGET SURVEY PARTICIPANTS

When selecting survey participants, review the list of organizations identified during your library manager interviews (chapter 5) and refer back to your compensation philosophy. Consider other libraries and other local organizations that hire your former employees and those you use as a pool from which to draw job candidates. Think locally, regionally, and nationally, as appropriate, for the type of position. Think library, educational institutions, nonprofits, public sector, and private sector, again depending upon the position and your competition for qualified applicants. For a slightly structured approach to selecting participants, brainstorm with the committee to complete worksheet 11.

Your selection of survey recipients will depend upon the labor market in your community and your direct competitors for human resources. For example, one library system included a number of local hospitals and health-care systems as participants, as they were "the employer of choice" for nonexempt staff and certain professional positions due to their flextime and other benefits. Therefore, it became important to obtain information about the pay practices, benefits, and salaries of those institutions.

Seek an appropriate balance between libraries and other competitors for employees. About 75 percent of the recipients of public library surveys are other public libraries. When working with academic libraries, 75 percent of those surveyed are other academic libraries, the local school board, and one or two public libraries. This has yielded an excellent response rate from the libraries surveyed (at least 75 to 80 percent or more return), approximately 65 to 75 percent from school boards and other public institutions, and about 20 to 50 percent from private companies. Because the response rate is typi-

cally lower from private organizations, it is best to design a separate, shorter survey that contains only general industry benchmark jobs (e.g., secretary, clerk, accountant, information technology specialist, department manager) and does not use library jargon.

How many organizations should you survey? A good rule of thumb is to survey twelve to fifteen libraries, public sector, or nonprofit organizations and five to eight private companies. Remember,

not every organization will respond

not all respondents will be able to match (that is, provide data for) every surveyed job

you can augment the data, especially data for the generic nonexempt and exempt positions, from published sources (See step 6, later in this chapter.)

Like you, potential participants are very busy and often receive many requests to participate in salary surveys. They will want to evaluate the cost and benefit of investing their time to complete the survey. To help increase participation, determine an appropriate contact in advance. For libraries, you can use your professional network. For general-industry participants, contact your local chapter of the Society for Human Resource Management or World at Work (formally known as the American Compensation Association). For public-sector connections, call the local chapter of the International Personnel Management Association, National Association of Counties, or International City Management Association, or just call the organization and ask for the human resources director. Capitalize on your contacts and network. If you know someone from a library association committee or even a nonprofit board you serve on, give that person a call.

Prior to mailing the survey, call the person yourself or ask someone in your library who has had prior contact or dealings with the organization to call and solicit participation. Let the person know that the survey is coming and why participation is important and appreciated.

Send the survey both electronically and by mail. Offer to receive responses in the way that is easiest for the participant—mail, fax, or e-mail. If nec-

Survey of Positions and Types of Employers

Library Positions	Type of Employer to Survey	Organization to Survey	Contact Name
Nonexempt Circulation Administrative support Accounting	*Local* City government County government School board Hospitals Local college/community University Private companies Health care		
Professional Accounting/finance Human resources Marketing	*Local, some regional* City government County government School board Hospitals Local college/community University Nonprofits For-profit companies Libraries		
Librarian Entry level MLS Experienced MLS Branch manager I, II Specialist Children's Technology Trainer Catalog Department Manager	*Local, regional, some national* Public libraries College libraries School board Special libraries		

essary, offer to meet with the participant and work through the survey face-to-face. This will also help ensure the reliability of job matching.

Offer participants a report (summary of findings) at the conclusion of the survey. You might also offer respondents something more tangible such as a T-shirt from your summer reading program, tickets to a fundraiser, membership in your Friends program or book group, etc. There is no ethical reason not to do so, and you know how

guilty some people feel when the American Whatever Association sends those mailing labels.

STEP 4
DECIDE IF YOU WILL ASK ABOUT PAY PRACTICES OR BENEFITS

As previously mentioned, base salary is only one aspect of total compensation. You may also want to ask questions about incentives and benefits. You might wonder, "Why even ask about incentives if we don't really have the ability to offer them?" Since general industry and even some government jurisdictions offer other cash awards (e.g., the city of Baltimore now offers incentives for certain positions, as do departments of the University of Maryland), you will want to be aware of this trend and have an idea of how it affects the total compensation package offered. You can obtain this information by asking:

Are employees in the position eligible for an incentive?

If so, what percent of base salary are they eligible to earn?

What is the average earned?

You might have a similar feeling about whether to ask about benefits, especially if you are tied to the university, college, or county government and are not able to make independent decisions about the benefits offered. Nonetheless, some library systems want a true picture of total compensation that includes both salaries and benefits; competitive information about salaries is sufficient for others.

In addition, while you might not have any control over the design of your benefit plans, you may use the knowledge you gain to

"lobby" for changes to your benefit plans in the future

inform employees about the value of benefits to them (often library benefits are very generous)

determine if the value of benefits offered by your competitors (whether they be much richer or less generous than yours) should be a factor in the level of pay you offer to employees

In some instances benefits are worth a substantial amount—sometimes as much as $2,000 to $4,000 per year *over* those offered by competitors. Because the cost of benefits has escalated so dramatically in recent years, a couple of things might happen:

Libraries may not be able to continue to absorb such large health-care premium increases

and may need to begin increasing the percentage of the employee contribution.

Even with price-shifting modifications to existing employer/employee contribution rates, benefits will continue to serve libraries as an invaluable tool for recruitment and retention—especially if employees can spend benefit dollars in a flexible manner.

Survey for benefits data only if you will use the information. It is a major undertaking for both the library commissioning the survey and for respondents. That is, reporting benefits information is time-consuming for respondents, and inputting and analyzing benefits information will take almost as much time as the salary segment of the study.

If you do decide to ask about pay practices and benefits, you will want to ask about the respondents'

job evaluation system

salary structure

basis for merit or performance adjustments (performance appraisal or automatic step), frequency, and size of increase

COLA increases and their frequency and amounts

bonus or other incentive/award plans

salary differentials or other pay practices for compensating staff assigned to work evenings, weekends, or holidays

STEP 5
DESIGN THE SURVEY

Keep the following basic design principles in mind when preparing the survey questionnaire. Although they might sound like little things, they do make a difference.

The final questionnaire should be easy to read, easy to respond to, and look appealing. You want respondents to want to flip through it for an overview, then take the time to read it in more detail.

Include information about your library system as well as an organization chart.

Make it look professional.

Number the pages.

Keep the size of the survey, including the number of positions and other questions, reasonable and not overwhelming.

Ask for participants' names and telephone numbers and include yours.

Underline or **otherwise highlight** key words.

Note in your cover letter if you have additional or open-ended questions at the end of the survey.

Design your data collection format (Excel spreadsheet or other) to parallel your questionnaire. (This will facilitate data entry and analysis.)

Pilot test your survey with your own data *before* you mail it.

The questionnaire should ask the following for each benchmark job:

base salary   Ask for the average/actual salary for a position as of a certain date. This number represents the current salary being paid to incumbents in a given position. If there is only one person in the position, the number is the individual's actual salary. If there are multiple staff in a position, this number will represent the average of their combined salaries. Many public and academic libraries, school boards, public jurisdictions, and nonprofits have a fiscal year that begins July 1. If this is the case in your situation, it makes sense to ask for data effective on that date.

salary range   Request the minimum, midpoint, and maximum of the salary range to which the position is assigned. While the average or median of all base salaries reported for each position is referred to as the "market rate," the range helps verify the lowest and highest actual base salary paid and will provide a good measure of how respondents are paying in relationship to their range. Keep in mind, though, that pay ranges are reflections of the policies and compensation philosophy of other organizations, which might or might not reflect your own.

type of job match   Ask participants to report if their job is "bigger than," "equal to," or "smaller than" your job summary (expressed in percentages: between 20 percent smaller and 20 percent larger than yours) and to describe the difference on a separate sheet so you can determine if the percentage difference is appropriate. Your summary job descriptions and cover letter will indicate the "scope measures," so the differences should not be difficult for respondents to provide.

other position information   You should request the following additional information for each position: the job title used in the respondent's organization, hours worked each week, number of incumbents, exempt or nonexempt status, union status, and size indicators (total number of employees, branches, and budget).

Think about what you really need to know and how this data will be helpful to you. Don't ask questions that fall into the "nice to know" category but whose answers won't necessarily be used for your project. Remember, the participation rate will be adversely affected if the questionnaire is too lengthy or cumbersome to complete.

In your instructions make it clear that participants should read and understand the job summaries provided and what is involved in the job in your organization before matching it to the surveyed jobs. Explain that they should not rely solely on title, because organizations use titles differently. One organization's administrative assistant is a $28,000-per-year support person, while another's is a $42,000 executive assistant. One public library in Maryland refers to employees holding a bachelor's degree who have completed the state's training program as "librarian," while others will only use that title for employees who hold a master's degree. Know how the job fits into the respondent's organization structure, to whom a person in that job reports, whether and how many the job holder supervises, and what education and experience are required to do the job competently. In summary, job matches are based on *job content,* including:

education and experience requirements of the job

scope (budget size, number of employees, or other scope data appropriate to the position)

breadth of job

supervisory responsibilities

They are *not* based on

title

current grade

incumbent salary

incumbent performance

market considerations

If the respondent's job matches at least 85 percent of your job summary, then it's probably a good match to include in the survey and in your subsequent analysis.

Approval

Once you have designed a complete draft of the survey, you will need to have the appropriate people (the library director, an employee committee, or both) review it. Your focus during the approval process should be to

- ensure that position summaries are accurate and that they represent the actual work being performed and the minimum qualifications for the job rather than what skills the incumbent might possess
- minimize the number of jobs surveyed (It's all too easy to keep adding just one or two jobs to the total list. Over time, this can have the unexpected outcome of making your survey too lengthy to expect a good participation rate.)

You can reduce the time spent on final approval processes if you seek review from the committee electronically. Since this is a critical point where there is much lost time, *set a return date* and adhere to it. Giving the members of the committee a few days to a week should be a sufficient amount of time to review the changes.

While the committee is reviewing the survey you can concentrate on the following administrative tasks:

- Verify your contact list and ensure that the appropriate people are contacted and informed about the survey.
- Prepare envelopes for mailing.
- Set up your data collection file (whether it be a spreadsheet or database application), and input your library's data, in advance, for comparative purposes later.

Pilot Test

Once the survey has been designed, reviewed by the appropriate parties, and approved, pilot test it. Have human resources, the assistant director, or your finance director complete the survey as a respondent. This step serves as the final check before the survey is distributed to other organizations. Upon completing the survey your internal respondents will be able to tell you about any glitches or problems they encountered during completion. Final changes and revisions to ensure ease of completion can then be made before your external market attempts to complete the survey. Please do not minimize the importance of pilot testing the survey *before* mailing it out. This is the time to make sure that the survey is easy to understand and complete, flows easily, and gives you what you need without too much work by participants.

Cover Letter

You will also need to draft a cover letter to go along with the survey itself. Let participants know why you are contacting them, provide some background information about your library, and inform them of the due date for their data. Don't forget to provide phone, fax, and e-mail contact information if participants have questions and to allow them to provide their responses by their method of choice.

Ask survey participants to respond within two weeks. Experience proves that the majority will take longer, so allow time for this in your project work plan. Plan to follow up with phone calls during the beginning of the third week after the survey is distributed.

STEP 6
USE OTHER MARKET
DATA SOURCES

So far you have read about the information you will need to collect for a special custom survey—a survey designed to meet *your* specifications and time line. There are, however, other ways to obtain information on what employers pay for jobs.

Published Surveys

Participating in or purchasing published surveys may be less expensive than conducting one of your own either independently or through consultants. They will, however, be more generic and less focused on your specific jobs or market for employees. You may need to find a number of surveys to adequately cover all of the library's benchmark positions. Given the competitive marketplace of today, you should not consider using a survey that is older than two years. For information technology and other difficult-to-recruit jobs, the data can become outdated even more quickly. Depending on what is available in your local area and the extent to which you are able to conduct market pricing research, a few sources for published data follow. Note that some can be expensive.

The Department of Labor, Bureau of Labor Statistics (BLS), provides good salary data on library and nonlibrary jobs alike. The data is available and can be sorted by region or metropolitan area, so you should be able to find data in geographic proximity. Be sure to note the date of the data provided, as BLS is typically one to three years behind. The data is still usable, but it will need to be aged (typically about 2.5 to 3 percent per year) to account for cost of living adjustments and other salary range increases applied industrywide. In addition, published surveys are available for purchase from such entities as the Economic Research Institute, Mercer, Hay, Abbott-Langer, and Price Waterhouse.

Telephone/Fax/E-Mail Surveys

The library world is a nicely networked market. You could design a brief survey where you need to know limited information on a few jobs such as one conducted on behalf of a public library client in the Northeast. A year following the implementation of a major new pay program, management wanted to follow up to make sure they were still on track with their entry-level salary for newly minted MLS librarians. Therefore, a brief survey was faxed to library systems included in the original survey, asking for returns within one week and offering the options of returning completed surveys electronically, via fax, or over the telephone. This garnered 100 percent participation. Participants' reports were prepared and sent to all respondents, even though it was just a small, quick survey.

Recruiting Ads or
Calls/Job Applications

You can go to local employers and ask for an application for a friend and ask a few questions about starting salary or benefits while you are there. This is a quick way of getting information that would be difficult to obtain by survey. This method should be used to verify or corroborate information you have, rather than as a primary source.

Industry- and Professional-
Group Surveys

These surveys are designed and conducted by professional, marketing, or recruiting groups or others. The American Library Association, state library associations, and other industry professional associations often survey constituents and make that information available. These are generally good sources of salary data for specific jobs of interest to a certain industry. Check with your local universities or colleges because they may produce salary surveys as well. The College and University Personnel Association (CUPA) publishes a survey that academic libraries might find useful. Also check with your human resources staff or the human resources staff at the college, university, city, or county level. These individuals often belong to professional organizations such as the Society for Human Resource Management or local or regional chapters thereof that often produce annual salary surveys. Finally, local or statewide organizations, such as your state library association, association of counties, or a municipal league, may produce salary surveys.

Keep in mind that salaries and benefits from respondents will often vary based on the size of organization and sector of the economy. For example, it is likely that the pay rates for a small public library will be lower than those of a university academic library. Likewise, the academic library rates will be lower than those of a local utility company. If you decide to include a professional association survey in your data, contact the survey sponsor and learn as much about it as possible. If you can't get answers to your questions, be careful how you use the data.

Be leery of a variety of surveys published by information technology, marketing, human resources, and finance groups as well. While many of them may look terrific, they may not be valid sources of salary information. If a survey doesn't include background on how the survey was conducted, publish a participant list or effective date of the data collected, or outline quality control standards and procedures for cleaning data, you can't consider the data valid.

Web Sites of Potential Participants

Often, when there is a lack of participation in a key area, say community colleges or local hospitals, you can research and find useful salary information on their Web sites. Some organizations publish their entire salary and grade structures and provide job descriptions online, ensuring that you will be able to make quality matches. Take this information with a grain of salt, however, because without speaking directly with someone in the human resources department, you can't be sure if it's truly up-to-date or if the organization is hiring (as common practice) well above range minimum, etc.

Be very wary of collecting salary data from the Internet unless it is from a reputable and reliable source. You will be able to find a salary for any position you can dream of on the Web, but ask yourself these questions.

Is this data from your geographic area?

What organizations are included? (Libraries? Fortune 500 companies?)

What are the budgets of these organizations?

How many employees do they have?

Are they comparable to your library?

Can you match a job description or position summary to one in your library? Does it include differentiation for years of experience or education required?

Not all information found on the Internet is questionable; however, make sure the information is really a match before incorporating it into your findings.

STEP 7
FOLLOW UP AND VERIFY RESPONSES

Not only will you need to follow up by calling the organizations to remind them to participate, you will need to contact them to help you "clean" the data after they complete and return your survey. Cleaning the data is almost literally just that. You need to review the data sent by survey participants and "clean it up." For example, if the respondent reported annual rates and you want hourly, you will need to convert the data to your hourly format (if you know their hours worked per week). If the respondent writes that their job is about equal to yours, yet it pays 50 percent more, you should call and verify the match or the numbers provided. Similarly, call to find out the true numbers if the respondent put the same number (salary data) in the columns headed minimum, midpoint, and average. It is important to thoroughly review all data to make sure it fits and makes sense and that, to the fullest extent possible, all information requested is provided.

Mistakes in data entry can happen. You need to check responses for reasonableness. That is, does the data make sense? If the response indicates that circulation assistants are earning more than the branch manager, you will need to follow up to ascertain the accuracy of the response. An error may be as simple as a participant's typo; however, the only way to be sure is to speak directly to someone from the organization.

Essentially, you should review the data at least twice. (You will end up reviewing it many more times.) First, each respondent's questionnaire should be thoroughly reviewed position by position, looking for inconsistencies. Second, after the data is entered into a spreadsheet, it should be reviewed position by position. (See figure 7.1.)

Generate a list of questions, if any, for each respondent, so you can make just one follow-up call during which you verify responses, review matches, and discuss reasons for particularly high or low rates of pay. Sometimes the respondents made an error; other times there are legitimate reasons for what appear to be inconsistencies. An example comes from a public library in Maryland. In reviewing its data, the consultant noticed that the actual and average salaries paid to many incumbents were close to, at, or over the maximum of their reported pay range.

FIGURE 7.1 Sample Spreadsheet for Capturing Data

Position: Librarian

Respondent	Average/Actual Salary	Number of Incumbents
Your Library	**$44,820**	2
Library E	$45,000	5
Library F	$41,515	1
Library B	$37,869	10
Library I	$37,800	50
Library D	$37,000	4
Library H	$36,705	2
Library A	$33,300	8
Company G	$30,000	4
Company C	$29,200	14
Total		100
Unweighted mean	$37,321	
Weighted mean	$36,289	
Median	$37,400	
Data range	$29,200 to $45,000 (or $15,800)	
Rank (your library)	2 of 10	
25th percentile	$32,475	
75th percentile	$42,341	

After a review and conversation with the library's contact, it was discovered that its ranges were particularly narrow (e.g., 35 percent for senior level positions) and many of its employees were long-service. These items explained what appeared at the outset to be inconsistencies.

STEP 8
ANALYZE AND ADJUST DATA

Figure 7.2 is a sample Excel spreadsheet for entering and analyzing the data that has additional formulas for aging data to a consistent date. Regardless of what method you choose to input your data, keep it fairly simple and focus on a few meaningful figures such as the following:

mean   the average of all of the data points. It treats each respondent's data the same, regardless of number of incumbents.

weighted mean   each respondent's data is "weighted" by the number of incumbents in the position; therefore, salary data from respondents with many incumbents in the position will have a greater influence on the weighted mean than will respondents with few incumbents.

median   the value where half the data is higher and half is lower. This measure minimizes the influence of extremes and is generally considered to be one of the most useful measures in compensation unless there is a specific reason not to use it.

data range   shows the salary data from high to low. This gives an indication of how dispersed the data is.

A number of other statistical tools are available to aid in analysis.

Do *not* include your own organization's data with others in the analysis initially. As in figure 7.2 your data should be shown for comparative purposes separately, by placing it in the first or last line. The spreadsheet shown in figure 7.2 can easily be adapted for your needs. You may want to change requested data or column headings to suit your needs.

FIGURE 7.2 Sample Spreadsheet for Analyzing Data

PUBLIC LIBRARIAN

Respondent Agency	Minimum Education	Degree of Match	Rationale	Number of Employees in Position	Number of Hours/ Week	Raw Data					Adjusted Data				
						Average Actual Pay	Minimum of Pay Range	Midpoint of Pay Range	Maximum of Pay Range	Longevity	Degree of Match	Average Actual Pay	Minimum of Pay Range	Midpoint of Pay Range	Maximum of Pay Range
Your library	MLS			13		$33,072	$25,526	$32,955	$39,195		1.00	$33,072	$25,526	$32,955	$39,195
Library 1	MLS	equal		18	37.5	40,619	30,401	35,139	39,878	$45,864	1.00	40,619	30,401	35,139	39,878
Community college 1	MA/S/L	+20%	Broader scope	4	40.0	49,920	30,700	52,958	75,216		0.80	39,936	24,560	42,366	60,173
Library 2	BA/BS	-10%	Education	5	37.5	28,490	27,008	33,755	40,502		1.10	31,339	29,709	37,131	44,552
Library 3	MLS	equal		29	40.0	28,413	24,960	28,891	31,866	38,730	1.00	28,413	24,960	28,891	31,866
Local school board	MLS	equal					31,721	38,861	46,000		1.00		31,721	38,861	46,000
Library 4	MLS	equal				42,768	32,243	42,768	53,293		1.00		32,243	42,768	53,293
Average (excluding your library)						$38,042	$29,506	$38,729	$47,793	$42,297		$35,077	$28,932	$37,526	$45,960
Variance % over/under average						-13%	-13%	-15%	-18%	-100%		-6%	-12%	-12%	-15%
Median (excluding your library)						$40,619	$30,551	$37,000	$43,251	$42,297		$35,638	$30,055	$37,996	$45,276
Variance % over/under median						-19%	-16%	-11%	-9%	-100%		-7%	-15%	-13%	-13%

The columns in figure 7.2 provide places to record the following information:

Column 1: name of respondent

Column 2: minimum education required of the incumbent to perform the job in a satisfactory manner

Column 3: degree of match—Remember, all who were surveyed were asked the degree, from 20 percent less to 20 percent more, to which their position matched your library's job.

Column 4: rationale to substantiate the degree of match—You want to know the basis upon which the respondent's position was deemed to be bigger or smaller than your own. Oftentimes the discrepancies are based on different educational requirements, years of experience, or supervisory status.

Column 5: number of employees in each position

Column 6: hours in the work week

Column 7: actual (if single incumbent) or average (for positions with multiple incumbents) pay in each job surveyed

Columns 8–10: minimum, midpoint, and maximum of the pay range to which the job is assigned

Column 11: amount of longevity pay, if any, awarded to employees with specified amounts of seniority or tenure with the library

The next section of columns (adjusted data) provides for the same information, as adjusted. Data would be adjusted to

ensure that all data is as of or effective to the same date

allow for a differential such as for education, supervisory responsibility, scope of work

provide a geographic differential, if appropriate

The formulas that have been entered will do the remainder of your work. For each position, it will calculate the average and median of each position (average/actual, minimum, midpoint, and maximum) as well as the percent variance of your library's data. This activity will give you excellent information about the relationship of your library's compensation to what is offered by those in your market. (See the Adjustments to Survey Data section following.)

Adjustments to Survey Data

Survey data may be "adjusted" to reflect differences between the library's job and respondents' jobs. This is a perfectly legitimate compensation practice. Some reasons for doing so include

scope of the job your organization or job covers more or less than the scope reported by respondents

level respondent's job is at a higher or lower level in the organization than your job (e.g., your job reports to a branch manager and the respondent's job reports to the assistant library director)

required knowledge your job requires more or less education or knowledge to do the job (knowledge and experience are generally strongly correlated with market pay levels)

breadth of responsibility the job in your library has different responsibilities from respondent's (e.g., the job for which you surveyed also supervises staff and respondent's job does not)

impact on organization outcomes the job for which you surveyed has more or less impact on the library than that of the respondent (For example, the position of marketing director in your library system might include responsibilities for public relations, marketing, fundraising, Friends of the Library, and working with the library's foundation, while in another library system, the incumbent is responsible only for public information.)

market demands new technology or "hot skills" (e.g., fund development, children's librarian), for example, have made the position more highly valued

In general, you would not make an adjustment to market data of more than +/– 20 percent. You should make very few, if any, at this level. Most of the adjustments you make should not exceed 10 percent. (A framework for adjustments is provided in figure 7.3.) In addition, adjusting data is also part of the art-versus-science aspect of compensation, as it can be subjective. However, once the percentage of adjustment is identified, it should be kept consistent throughout data analysis. For example, if you choose to adjust data by 10 percent for a position for which you require a master's degree, but the minimum qualification for some respondents is a bachelor's degree, then maintain the 10 percent educational differential throughout.

Hybrid Jobs

In the past, jobs were created using a homogenized hierarchy—jobs devoted to one functional area and expertise were organized from department head down to clerical or blue-collar jobs. Whether it's due to the unique needs of your library, the specific capabilities of certain employees, or the desire to

---

FIGURE 7.3   Framework for Adjusting the Data

+/− 5 to 10 percent

Just noticeably different

Nonexempt position versus supervisory level

One level movement in career path or job family

Where added responsibility is less valuable than the core job

Education level—Typically add or subtract 10 percent for MS versus BS and 5 percent for BS versus AA, although this also depends on accompanying years of experience (i.e., AA with 4 years' experience might equal a BS)

Supervisory responsibility—Adjustments could be made for differences in numbers of people supervised (i.e., 15 versus 5)

Levels of experience—Position requires more or less previous or related experience than benchmark job

---

+/− 10 to 15 percent

Supervisory or lower management jobs—Double or half of scope measures or level of responsibility (e.g., number of employees supervised, number of branches)

Supervisor versus manager or director versus manager

Supervises professional-level positions

Upper management jobs—Double or half of scope measures (e.g., revenues, large differences in budget, number of branches, collections)

Significant difference in levels of experience—Position requires much more or much less previous experience than benchmark job

---

+/− 15 to 20 percent

Significantly different

Director versus executive

For senior managers—Double or half of scope measures (e.g., budget, number of branches, collections)

For senior managers—Added responsibility is less valuable than the core job

---

capitalize on interests and provide new challenges, many jobs are beginning to be designed in a nontraditional way. In today's world, the hybrid job—those jobs that *regularly* consist of work in more than one functional area—is becoming more the rule than the exception. There are three possible approaches for market pricing hybrid jobs:

majority approach   Where more than 50 percent of the job is an identifiable function, price the job based on that major portion of the job. This is especially appropriate if the other portions of the job are of equivalent degree of difficulty or have about the same market value.

weighting approach   This approach is appropriate when you prefer to acknowledge the different aspects of a job by pricing and weighting its component parts. (See worksheet 8 in chapter 6.) For example, if a job is 70 percent financial analyst and 30 percent accountant, take 70 percent of the average actual salary data for a financial analyst and add to it 30 percent of the average actual salary data for an accountant to determine the going rate for your hybrid job.

highest value approach   Where you are competing for technical talent or other in-demand expertise, market price the entire job based on the portion attributable to the highest market rate. Do this regardless of the percentage of time spent on that task. For example, for the financial analyst/accountant, you would market price the job as that of a financial analyst.

Note that the value of the job is *not* cumulative. Don't simply add up the market value of both jobs to get the combined value of the job. In addition, minor add-on functions with market values less than the highest market value don't increase the value of the job being priced.

STEP 9
PREPARE AND SEND REPORTS

The final report of your findings and results should conform to your library's style for its other reports (for example, summarized versus fully detailed). Attempt to present only the most useful and descriptive data, which will be different depending upon the audience. On the one hand, the more information included in your final report, the more questions that may arise about what data is more valuable. In addition, each constituency will view what is valuable differently. On the other hand, you want to provide enough information so that informed, intelligent decisions can be made. It is perhaps best not to give anyone but the project manager the line-by-line data, but do provide summaries by category of position: e.g., nonexempt, exempt, management. As discussed in chapter 2, get input and buy-in during the initial stages of the project on what the report should include. Generally, your report should

- include an executive summary
- be consistent
- be well documented
- be attractive and easy to read (perhaps with bar or line graphs)

This report should include summarized results of the survey and be brief but meaningful. The report should be promptly sent to all participants who responded to your survey after your final report has been presented to the board. Include your name and telephone number in case there are any questions. When preparing the participants' reports, don't give specifics or break confidentiality. In other words, provide summary data, not individual data points identifying what respondents are paying. Use averages or means, highs and lows, etc. Make sure that you've provided enough information to be useful to those who took the time to provide you with their salary and other data.

8

Salary Structure Design

Now that you have market data and a hierarchical ordering of positions, it's time to do something with this information and design your salary structure. Salary structures consist of jobs of roughly equal value or worth that are grouped into grades with competitive salary ranges. Pay (or salary) ranges express rates from the bottom to top or from minimum to maximum of each grade. The pay range represents a group of jobs. The intent of having salary ranges is to put limits on the lowest and highest rates your library will pay for any given job. Positions are assigned to grades, and pay ranges are based on job content and/or market value and/or internal equity (*not* on employee value or individual performance).

Each salary range includes a minimum, midpoint, and maximum, with the midpoint representing the market or "going rate" for the job. The minimum is the least amount, and the maximum is the most an employee should be earning for the job. Figures 8.1 and 8.2 show two examples of salary structures.

FIGURE 8.1   Salary Ranges for a University

Grade	Minimum	Midpoint	Maximum
1	$70,000	$105,000	$140,000
2	64,000	91,000	118,000
3	55,000	79,000	103,000
4	48,000	69,000	90,000
5	42,000	60,000	78,000
6	36,000	52,000	68,000
7	32,000	45,000	59,000
8	27,000	39,000	51,000
9	24,000	34,000	44,000
10	21,000	30,000	39,000

FIGURE 8.2
Salary Ranges for a Medium-Sized Public Library

Grade	Minimum	Midpoint	Maximum
1	$11,960	$14,472	$16,983
2	13,936	16,863	19,789
3	14,872	17,995	21,118
4	16,432	19,883	23,333
5	18,096	21,896	25,696
6	19,760	23,910	28,059
7	21,320	25,979	30,274
8	23,920	28,943	33,966
9	26,520	32,089	37,658
10	28,600	34,606	40,612
11	31,720	38,381	45,042
12	33,800	40,898	47,996
13	37,731	45,654	53,577
14	41,392	50,085	58,777
15	45,552	55,118	64,684
16	50,960	61,662	72,363

The first is the set of salary ranges developed for a university that has two major libraries—law and medicine. The second shows ranges developed for a medium-sized public library.

The pay structure is a tool for management and employees. Within policies that provide flexibility for making pay-related decisions, managers need guidelines to ensure organizational consistency, and employees need to know that pay will be equitable and competitive. Although the pay structure is a tool, adherence to it should not be so rigid that responses to a changing environment and opportunities to reward, recruit, or retain your most highly productive employees are difficult to make or ignored.

You now have all the data you need to prepare your salary structure: information obtained through job analysis, job evaluation, and market review and analysis. Armed with this information, a number of steps are generally followed. This chapter provides a discussion of these steps along with additional information on

clustering jobs to create pay ranges

calculating range spreads

determining range progressions

identifying the number of grades

costing the salary structure

This chapter also contains examples of salary structures and compensation plans as well as sample spreadsheets to help you design your salary ranges and calculate the costs to implement your new program.

DEVELOPING PAY RANGES

The first step in developing pay ranges is to compile all of the salary data into one chart, allowing you to look at the big picture. First, group together jobs with similar value to the library based upon points (chapter 6), similar market data (chapter 7), or a combination of the two to determine salary grades.

Determine Variance

The variance, or difference, between the market data and your library's data is best expressed as a percentage. This number will show the relationsip of each of your positions to the market, either as a positive number (above the market) or a negative number (below the market). To calculate a variance, divide your salary data for a given position by the average or median salary data for the same position in the market, then subtract 1 from the total. For example

(your data/market average or market median) – 1 = % variance

Review the following example from ABC Library for an entry-level librarian position:

ABC actual/average salary = $32,500

Market average salary = $34,750

($32,500 / $34,750) = .935

.935 – 1 = –.065 or –6.5%

ABC's job is 6.5 percent behind the market's actual/average salary for the same position.

Why subtract *1*? It may seem odd, but adding this extra step allows you to clearly see the variance, –6.5 percent in the example, versus having to do the calculation in your head (.935 minus 1 is .065 or 6.5 percent less than 100 percent—the market value for the job). This formula is easily entered into an Excel spreadsheet such as the one shown in figure 8.3. Figure 8.3 is a market analysis, showing all positions and salary data collected for the ABC Library. The spreadsheet shows major data points—market hourly actual/average, market midpoint, market minimum, and market maximum—and compares them with the same points for ABC Library. Note, however, that the cells showing the variance will need to be formatted to express their result as a percentage. Another important note: this calculation will work for any of the salary data comparison points—actual/average, minimum, midpoint, and maximum. Just be sure to compare apples to apples—that is, compare the same data point in your library to that of the market.

Set up the Spreadsheet

When setting up the spreadsheet in Excel (figure 8.3), link the market analysis to the salary data spreadsheets (see chapter 7) for each position. Linking is an Excel function that automatically updates data to all linked sheets when changes are made to the source sheet. In other words, if you link the market analysis sheet to the individual salary sheets, any changes made to the salary data sheets (adding a participant's data, for instance) will automatically be reflected in the market analysis, eliminating the need to duplicate efforts.

You will notice that the salaries in figure 8.3 are reflected as hourly figures. Many libraries find this a more useful comparison than annual salaries—some use a combination of both. This decision is entirely up to you; however, if you use an hourly figure, be sure you know how many hours per week each position works (a question usually asked in a market survey—see chapter 7). Many full-time library positions represent a 35-hour workweek, some a 37.5-hour workweek, and others a 40-hour workweek. If you gather this information, you can trans-

late the hourly figure to an accurate annual one if necessary and ensure a valid comparison to your annual figures.

Review Results

After you have determined the variance from the market for each position, review the results. For example, the first job shown in figure 8.3 is circulation clerk. Reading across, you can see that ABC's actual or average salary is 5 percent ahead of the market average. The midpoint of ABC's salary range is 6 percent behind the market midpoint; and ABC's range minimum is 12 percent behind that of the market. (The variance from the market maximum is not shown on this sheet, but you could certainly conduct the same analysis for this data point.)

How can the actual or average pay be ahead of the market but the range be below it? Well, any number of hypotheses can be formed. Since actual/average pay is the actual (if only one incumbent in this position) or average (if multiple incumbents hold this position) pay received by employees in the position, high actual/average pay could indicate that the individuals in the position are long-term employees. While the salary range may not have been adjusted in quite a few years, actual employee salaries could have increased year after year, moving them toward range maximum. Along these same lines, remember that the data collected from other libraries and organizations does not typically account for years of experience. So, this data point could represent a group of circulation clerks that (on the whole) are new or newer employees and are therefore receiving pay at the beginning of their salary range. While it is important (depending on your philosophy) that actual/average pay be competitive with the market, the range minimum is also important because it has an impact on recruitment and will also have a heavy impact on implementation costs.

The market analysis data should then be sorted by median market average/actual pay from lowest to highest. However, it is again important to look at the big picture—at all data points—as well as to

FIGURE 8.3 Sample Library Market Analysis

Job Title	Median Market Average/ Actual	ABC Average/ Actual	% Variance	Median Market Midpoint	ABC Midpoint	% Variance	Median Market Minimum	ABC Minimum	% Variance	Median Market Maximum
Circulation clerk	$10.97	$11.57	5	$10.78	$10.12	-6	$ 9.27	$ 8.16	-12	$12.50
Processing clerk	11.15	10.98	-2	10.50	9.79	-7	9.15	7.98	-13	11.98
Interlibrary loan assistant	11.25	13.07	16	10.79	10.12	-6	9.62	8.16	-15	12.32
Administrative/office assistant	12.17	12.08	-1	10.79	10.12	-6	9.26	8.16	-12	14.37
Delivery driver	12.19	10.30	-16	11.44	8.91	-22	9.13	7.19	-21	13.57
Accounting clerk	13.77	12.89	-6	14.01	11.57	-17	10.69	10.98	3	15.24
Library associate I	14.77	13.98	-5	14.58	12.24	-16	12.15	11.32	-7	15.58
Library associate II	15.23	14.25	-6	15.07	13.17	-13	12.97	12.05	-7	16.64
Senior accounting clerk	15.66	19.82	27	16.02	15.35	-4	12.55	12.38	-1	20.00
Automation technician	16.25	14.80	-9	16.31	15.35	-6	12.52	12.38	-1	20.04
Librarian	16.32	16.02	-2	17.41	16.44	-6	14.73	14.22	-3	21.00
Office manager	16.34	19.82	21	14.73	15.35	4	11.08	12.38	12	18.32
Catalog librarian	17.41	17.12	-2	16.28	17.02	5	13.44	13.35	-1	18.53
Senior automation technician	18.21	17.84	-2	17.78	16.44	-8	16.02	14.22	-11	20.19
Manager, information services	23.66	20.28	-14	19.74	17.81	-10	16.54	14.36	-13	23.12
Assistant administrator	24.78	23.11	-7	24.83	29.54	19	26.75	26.51	-1	30.26
Library administrator	28.85	28.65	-1	26.93	30.38	13	22.36	24.50	10	32.57
Manager, automation services	28.92	28.70	-1	28.44	28.13	-1	22.14	22.68	2	35.39

consider the source of each to make a proper assessment of market competitiveness.

Cluster Jobs

Figure 8.4 shows the beginning of the formulation of data clusters, which will ultimately become salary ranges. Reviewing the market analysis, begin to group the positions into clusters. A cluster is a natural grouping of jobs based on job evaluation points (if used) and market data or a combination of both. These groupings will represent the first draft of your salary grades. You may eventually shift jobs in and out of these clusters based on internal equity issues, office politics, or other reasons, but for now, consider this the starting point for your salary structure.

It is difficult to say which data point is the most important for this clustering process. Since the midpoint represents the market, your midpoint should reflect salaries actually paid. Yet range design is important too. If recruitment is a major issue facing your library, then pay attention to the minimum of the range and hiring salaries. If there are many staff members at or near the range maximum, then survey findings about maximum pay should be highlighted. Again, job evaluation data and many other factors can have an impact on these decisions.

The columns in figure 8.4 show the following:

proposed range a number assigned to put the clusters in context; these numbers may change as you develop final salary ranges

job title

current grade a helpful data point to review, although it should not drive the placement of jobs into clusters unless one of your goals is not to stray far from the status quo

salary data (columns 4–10) data points brought over from the market analysis sheet, again, to provide context

cluster data (columns 11–16) after these jobs have been grouped into clusters, determine the average of each salary data point per cluster (This sheet does not limit the analysis to only one data point but shows several

that may be useful in ultimately designing ranges.)

variance (columns 12, 14, 16) differences from one cluster to the next expressed as a positive or negative percentage

Looking at cluster (or proposed range) 2, you can see that the average midpoint for this cluster is $10.79 per hour; the average actual salary per cluster is $11.46; and the average minimum is $9.38. This data represents only market data and does not include ABC's salary information. Once jobs have been grouped into clusters, rank the groups from high to low or vice versa based on whichever data point or points you've decided to focus upon.

You will notice that the spreadsheet in figure 8.4 does not exactly follow the order of positions in figure 8.3. This is perfectly acceptable and actually preferable. It is rare that a salary survey of current market data mirrors the library's values for internal equity, recruitment and retention issues, and financial abilities. While the market analysis spreadsheet in figure 8.3 shows the circulation clerk position as having the lowest market actual/average pay, in figure 8.4 ABC Library has identified the processing clerk position as its lowest level position based on pay.

It is clear that figure 8.4 is by no means a final product. There are differences that need to be "smoothed." Look, for example, at cluster 3—delivery driver. This position was placed in its own cluster because the market midpoint falls nicely between the clusters around it. It is a natural break to place this job here. However, when looking at the same clusters' salary range minimums, it becomes apparent that an adjustment will have to be made, as the market minimum is actually 3 percent less than the cluster before it.

Calculate Range Spreads

You are now ready to calculate a pay range for each grade. Assuming that the market rate for the job cluster is placed in the middle of the range (midpoint), establish a range spread. The spread should fit with the type of positions and the number of grades.

FIGURE 8.4 Sample Library Structure Design

Proposed Range	Job Title	Current Grade	Median Market Avg./Act.	ABC Avg./Act.	Median Market Midpoint	ABC Midpoint	Median Market Minimum	ABC Minimum	Median Market Maximum	Average Midpoint Per Cluster	% Variance from Previous Cluster	Average Avg./Act. Per Cluster	% Variance from Previous Cluster	Average Minimum Per Cluster	% Variance from Previous Cluster
1	Processing clerk	5	$11.15	$10.98	$10.50	$9.79	$9.15	$7.98	$11.98	$10.50		$11.15		$9.15	
2	Circulation clerk	6	10.97	11.57	10.78	10.12	9.27	8.16	12.50	10.79	3	11.46	3	9.38	3
	Interlibrary loan assistant	6	11.25	13.07	10.79	10.12	9.62	8.16	12.32						
	Administrative/office assistant	6	12.17	12.08	10.79	10.12	9.26	8.16	14.37						
3	Delivery driver	4	12.19	10.30	11.44	8.91	9.13	7.19	13.57	11.44	6	12.19	6	9.13	-3
4	Accounting clerk	8	13.77	12.89	14.01	11.57	10.69	10.98	15.24	14.01	22	13.77	13	10.69	17
5	Library associate I	9	14.77	13.98	14.58	12.24	12.15	11.32	15.58	14.66	5	15.55	13	11.62	9
	Office manager	12	16.34	19.82	14.73	15.35	11.08	12.38	18.32						
6	Library associate II	10	15.23	14.25	15.07	13.17	12.97	12.05	16.64	15.07	3	15.23	-2	12.97	12
7	Senior accounting clerk	12	15.66	19.82	16.02	15.35	12.55	12.38	20.00	16.20	8	16.44	8	12.84	-1
	Catalog librarian	15	17.41	17.12	16.28	17.02	13.44	13.35	18.53						
	Automation technician	12	16.25	14.80	16.31	15.35	12.52	12.38	20.04						
8	Librarian	14	16.32	16.02	17.41	16.44	14.73	14.22	21.00	17.59	9	17.26	5	15.38	20
	Senior automation technician	14	18.21	17.84	17.78	16.44	16.02	14.22	20.19						
9	Manager, information services	16	23.66	20.28	19.74	17.81	16.54	14.36	23.12	19.74	12	23.66	37	16.54	8
10	Assistant administrator	20	24.78	23.11	24.83	28.13	26.75	22.68	30.26	24.83	26	24.78	5	26.75	62
11	Library administrator	21	28.85	28.65	26.93	30.38	22.36	24.50	32.57	26.93	8	28.85	16	22.36	-16
12	Manager, automation services	20	28.92	28.70	28.44	28.13	22.14	22.68	35.39	28.44	6	28.92	0	22.14	-1

97

Range spreads are expressed as the percentage difference from the minimum to the maximum of a grade and are derived from the midpoint (market rate for a group of jobs). Following is an example calculation using a range spread of 50 percent and a range midpoint of $25,000.

To find the minimum, divide the midpoint by 1.25. Why 1.25? A range spread of 50 percent means that there will be a 50 percent difference between the minimum and maximum of the grade. Since range spreads are calculated from the midpoint, it follows that—since the midpoint is one-half the distance between the minimum and the maximum—there would be 25 percent difference between the minimum and the midpoint.

$$\text{range midpoint} / 1.25 = \text{range minimum}$$
$$\$25,000 / 1.25 = \$20,000$$

To find the maximum of the same pay grade, multiply the minimum (that you found previously) by 1.5. The desired difference between the minimum and maximum is 50 percent. So, once you have calculated the minimum, you can find the maximum of the pay grade by adding 50 percent to the minimum.

$$\text{range minimum} \times 1.5 = \text{range maximum}$$
$$\$20,000 \times 1.5 = \$30,000$$

Remember, the 50 percent range spread is just an example. You need to determine the most appropriate spread for your library system because it will have an impact upon hiring and retention costs. Therefore, you need to consider economic projections and the number of employees whose actual pay rates will fall below the minimum or above the maximum of their new salary range. If, for example, the salaries of many of your employees will fall below their new minimum or above the maximum of their new pay grade, one conclusion might be that the range spreads are too small or narrow.

For help in determining appropriate range spreads, in addition to the methods given, review the information received in your market survey data to see what spreads were reported by other organizations. To determine the spreads used by respondents, divide the range maximum by the minimum—for example, an answer of 1.25 means a spread of 25

percent. Don't forget that because you are working with averages as well as ranges, and because every organization has a potentially different structure, the spreads reported may be scattered from wide to narrow. However, you will be able to note trends and understand what other organizations are doing simply by analyzing the individual data reported.

Typically range spreads are more narrow at the lower pay grades of the library's structure and wider at the higher grades. This reflects several considerations: lower-level jobs are typically in grades with narrower spreads to avoid overpaying for what are usually more-defined, fairly stable, entry-level, nonprofessional positions. Senior-level jobs normally have wider range spreads to allow for professional development and job growth in managerial or other professional positions that may change and grow over time. It also takes a longer period of time—often several years—to learn jobs and achieve competency at senior levels; thus, it is expected that it will take longer to reach the midpoint or market rate for the job. Furthermore, jobs at the senior level are frequently evolving, allowing for job growth in a wider salary range. Finally, additional responsibilities, technologies, etc., may make these positions "worth" more to the library and, therefore, result in more dollars to the incumbent.

Determine Range Progression

After calculating your range spreads, determine the progression from grade to grade. While the range spread indicates the width of a grade from minimum to maximum, the range progression indicates the difference or "jump" from one grade to the next. Just as range spread is calculated from the midpoint, the progression of grades is also calculated from this data point.

It's important to keep in mind the anticipated increase from one grade to the next. This increment shouldn't be so small as to be inconsequential when an employee receives a promotion or takes a new job; however, it shouldn't be so large as to be financially impractical in advancing employees. Midpoint progressions typically range from 8 percent to 10 percent between grades at the lower end of the structure to more than 15 percent at the higher levels. The increment does *not* have to be consistent. That is, you do not need to design a structure with evenly spaced increases from one grade to another (e.g., 10 percent or *x* percent between all grades) or evenly progressing midpoints (10 percent, 10 percent, 11 percent, 11 percent, 12 percent, etc.) between the midpoints of each grade. Your midpoint progression, as always, will be a function of the market data and your compensation philosophy.

Typical range spreads and midpoint progression by employee category (nonexempt entry level, nonexempt technical and paraprofessional, professional and management) are shown in figure 8.5. The figure shows the typical range spreads and midpoint progressions for groups of jobs that usually cluster together in the same pay grades of a salary structure. For instance, the second category (nonexempt technical/paraprofessional) shows a fairly narrow range spread for circulation and clerical jobs because these jobs are normally well-defined and relatively routine and would not grow or develop significantly in terms of responsibilities; rather, an individual who has grown out of this position would be reclassified or promoted. Therefore, a narrow range spread is appropriate. The last two categories, however, show a much wider range spread. This wider spread takes into consideration the fact that these professional and managerial jobs may grow or develop, more responsibilities are likely to be added, or new skills

FIGURE 8.5 Typical Range Spreads by Employee Category

Employee Category	Range Spread (Minimum to Maximum)	Midpoint Progression (% from One Midpoint to the Next)
Nonexempt entry level Custodial and maintenance job families Pages Entry-level circulation staff	Narrow ranges (30%–35%)	7%–10%
Nonexempt technical/paraprofessional Circulation staff Clerical Library assistants and associates First-level supervisors	Relatively narrow ranges (35%–45%)	8%–12%
Professional Librarians Administrative Department heads Branch managers	Wider ranges (45%–60%)	12%–15%
Management Senior managers Director of finance Director of human resources Associate directors Deputy directors Library directors	Widest ranges (60% and wider)	15%–25%

could be learned and included in the positions without having to reclassify them. The room for growth and flexibility is built into the wider range.

Likewise the larger midpoint progressions at higher levels of the organization follow the same logic. A promotion from an entry-level circulation assistant to a senior circulation assistant may be an 8 percent increment, reflecting that the incumbent is performing basically the same duties and responsibilities in the senior position but has more experience or perhaps some lead-worker responsibilities. A promotion from librarian I to a branch manager, on the other hand, may represent a significant increase in responsibility and, therefore, is differentiated by a wider progression between these grades. Finally, it's important to note that the jobs grouped together in each row are not presented in hierarchical order, but rather as groups of jobs that share similar characteristics and would fall into similar grades in the salary structure.

Identify the Number of Grades

You may wonder how many grades the structure should have. The answer is simple: there is no right answer. The number of grades in your system depends on two major factors: the market data (salary data of competitors) findings and your organizational structure. If you have a flat structure (see figure 8.6, part A), with less rather than more levels of management and middle management, you will need fewer grades. If your pay ranges are wider and employees move through them based upon acquired skills and competencies, you will design a structure with fewer grades. If you currently have more levels of management and staff positions and your culture dictates the only way to increase base salary requires a move up in job family (a common practice in academic libraries and higher education in general) and a new title and grade are necessary (e.g., a system with three levels of library associate in three separate grades), you will need to have

FIGURE 8.6   Flat and Multilevel Organization Structures

A. Flat Organization Structure with Few Grades		B. Multilevel Organization Structure with Many Grades	
Grade	*Title*	*Grade*	*Title*
1	Page	1	Page
2	Circulation clerk	2	Circulation clerk I (entry level)
3	Circulation supervisor	3	Circulation clerk II (3 years' experience)
4	Library assistant	4	Circulation supervisor
5	Librarian		Library assistant I (entry level with bachelor's degree)
6	Manager (materials, cataloging, processing)	5	Library assistant II (bachelor's degree with state certification)
7	Branch manager (large branch), department heads	6	Library assistant II (bachelor's degree, state certification, and 4 years' experience)
8	Assistant director	7	Librarian I (entry-level, MLS)
9	Library director	8	Librarian II (MLS and 3 years' experience)
		9	Branch manager I (small branch)
		10	Manager (materials, cataloging, processing)
		11	Branch manager II (larger branch)
		12	Department head
		13	Assistant director
		14	Library director

more rather than fewer grades. See figure 8.6, part B, for a graphic example of this concept. It shows a deeper system with differentiation made among different levels in the same job title—library assistant and librarian, for example. This type of structure would usually be appropriate for a larger system that by its nature would have more staff, provide more services, and necessitate more positions. However, it could also work in a smaller system that wants to provide more opportunities for advancement and career progression for its employees.

Other considerations when determining the number of grades your structure will have include

> the number of skill or responsibility distinctions in your library system (Your job evaluation/point factor plan will indicate "natural breaks" by points, as will your own assessment of internal value.)
>
> the number of jobs in different job families
>
> room for appropriate differentiation in pay between supervisors and those they supervise
>
> administrative and political considerations

Experience with academic and public libraries has shown that—excluding the director's position—you will have no fewer than eight and should have no more than seventeen grades. The number of grades has to fit the organization and its structure, size, culture, and management philosophy—which differ from system to system. Generally, if your library hasn't conducted a study for a while, the possibility of eliminating or combining/collapsing some grades and having fewer grades with wider ranges is possible.

DRAFTING THE STRUCTURE

By now you will have reviewed and analyzed market data, grouped jobs into like clusters, calculated pay ranges for each new grade, and developed progressions from grade to grade. Figure 8.7 shows the development of the structure incorporating all previous activities to this point. The figure provides the following data:

> *grade number*   new grade numbers assigned to each cluster

> *title*   the position titles that are included in each salary grade
>
> *salary range*   the minimum, midpoint, and maximum salary for the range (shown both hourly and annually)
>
> *range spread*   the percent spread between minimum and maximum
>
> *midpoint progression*   the percent difference between range midpoints

In figure 8.7 the ordering of positions and the associated salary data have been further refined from the structure design (figure 8.4) to allow for a variety of factors, including internal equity, culture, the market, etc. You will also note that there are three empty or open grades at the beginning of the structure. ABC Library determined that the lowest possible salary it will pay for the positions it currently has is $9.15 an hour. However, what happens if this system decides in the future to hire pages or other lower level positions? The structure has been designed with some built-in flexibility that will allow ABC Library to place lower level jobs on the salary structure without conducting another study. You'll also notice that the delivery driver position is placed in grade 4 with the processing clerk. A review of market data showed that this position was actually paid higher in the market; however, for political and internal equity reasons, having the delivery driver in a higher grade than the processing clerk would not "fly" in this organization. Remember that after a pay plan is designed, approved, and implemented, you and everyone else in the library will have to live with it. In some instances, it may not be worth sticking strictly to the hierarchy the data shows if it goes too far against the grain of your culture or organization structure.

In figure 8.7 there is also an open grade at grade 12. Based on salary data and current position descriptions, it was determined that no position fits into this grade. However, it is left open because to move from the salary range of grade 11 to that of grade 13 would be a 25 percent jump—too large an increment from one grade to another at this level in this system. In the future, ABC Library may have another level of manager or may

FIGURE 8.7   Sample Public Library Salary Ranges

Grade	Title	Hourly/Annual			% Range Spread	% Midpoint Progression
		Minimum	*Midpoint*	*Maximum*		
1		$ 6.96 12,670	$ 8.18 14,888	$ 9.40 17,105	35	
2		7.49 13,631	8.80 16,016	10.11 18,401	35	8
3		8.16 14,857	9.59 17,457	11.02 20,057	35	9
4	Delivery driver Processing clerk	9.15 16,653	10.98 19,984	12.81 23,314	40	14
5	Interlibrary loan assistant Administrative/office assistant	10.21 18,586	12.51 22,768	14.81 26,950	45	14
6	Accounting clerk	11.34 20,631	13.89 25,273	16.44 29,915	45	11
7	Office manager Senior accounting clerk	12.36 22,488	15.14 27,547	17.92 32,607	45	9
8	Library associate I Automation technician	13.59 24,737	16.99 30,922	20.39 37,106	50	12
9	Library associate II Senior automation technician	14.78 26,892	18.47 33,615	22.16 40,338	50	9
10	Librarian Catalog librarian	16.55 30,119	20.69 37,649	24.82 45,179	50	12
11	Manager, information services	18.37 33,433	22.96 41,791	27.55 50,149	50	11
12		20.39 37,110	25.49 46,388	30.59 55,665	50	11
13	Manager, automation services Assistant administrator	22.95 41,769	29.17 53,089	35.39 64,410	54	14
	Library administrator	Off scale				

expand the grade 11 manager of information services position into a larger, more responsible position worthy of a different level of pay. On the other hand, the potential exists that employees in grade 11 will assume they can move into the open grade 12, so ABC Library needs to be mindful about how to communicate the meaning and intent of salary ranges with no positions assigned to them.

Take your time reviewing this information and designing the ranges. You probably will need several drafts before getting the right fit.

Nonbenchmark Jobs

Since not all jobs were market-priced, the remaining jobs need to be slotted into the salary scale. This can be done in one of two ways or a combination of both. First, if you established a hierarchical ordering of positions via the point factor process (chapter 6), you will have a point log indicating the number of levels and the number of points within each level. Simply slot each job into the appropriate salary grade with other jobs having a similar number of points. For example:

Number of Points	Salary Grade
0–100	1
101–200	2
201–300	3

The second method of slotting is just that: jobs are "slotted" into the system without point totals, often by the committee. This is based upon the value of each job compared with other jobs in the job family (e.g., if you placed a senior circulation assistant in a salary grade 4, you might slot a circulation supervisor into a salary grade 5 or 6 depending on the verifiable differences between both jobs) and/or the value of the job in relation to other jobs within the same grade (e.g., accounting clerk might be slotted in the same grade as circulation assistant because of the similar level and types of skill, effort, and responsibilities).

While going through the slotting process, remember to keep a differential of 10 percent to 20 percent between an individual contributor and that job's supervisor or manager. The size of this gap will differ if your organizational structure is flat or hierarchical or has few or many levels of supervision. The nature of the position (circulation supervisor in a branch or department head) and the type of work being performed (highly skilled or technical or more routine in nature) will also determine the differential.

To increase buy-in, you should consider including department heads, the members of the review committee, or the members of the evaluation subcommittee in the slotting process. As an alternative, invite them to review the final draft of the salary structure with all jobs either market priced or slotted into grades before submitting the draft for final review and approval.

Sample Salary Structures

Examples of salary structures that show the assignment of all library positions to a salary grade follow as figures 8.8 and 8.9. Keep in mind that these structures were custom designed to meet the specific needs and internal and external conditions facing the library systems at the time. Each was designed in consideration of the value of certain positions to the system in meeting institutional goals, fiscal constraints, staffing needs, training opportunities, the difficulty attracting and retaining employees, and so forth.

The structure presented in figure 8.8 has at its foundation a large, custom market study and the creation of an internal job-worth hierarchy developed with a whole-job ranking system. Senior management was quite involved in providing input and review at the appropriate times. This structure shows the job titles in alphabetical order that were grouped into each grade and the associated salary range. The structure was presented to this library's board in this simplified format; you could certainly modify the format to suit your needs by adding the midpoint of each range, showing hourly rates, and so forth. In this example, the director is contractual and does not have a salary range; the salary for this position is determined by the board and is not included in the salary structure.

The library in figure 8.8 is financially sound and in a fund-raising, construction, and renovation mode. Included in its constituency are many sophisticated library users and researchers. The system stays up to date with new technology and trains staff appropriately and often. Individuals with MLS degrees, including those with a specialized focus, are highly valued in this system, and they are paid accordingly, as is reflected in the salary structure.

The salary structure for a smaller library (shown in figure 8.9), with four small branches and two storefront locations, was developed using a combination of point factor and market data. In this example you can see that the emphasis is on library assistants (with a high school degree plus experience) who perform circulation duties and the day-to-day functions of customer service. Branches are managed by library associates (with a bachelor's degree plus experience). The assistant director and library director are the only library personnel who hold MLS degrees. The director of this system supervises approximately thirty-seven employees and is responsible for many of the external and policy-making functions, and the assistant director handles

FIGURE 8.8   Salary Structure of a Medium-Sized Public Library Based on Market Data and Whole-Job Ranking

Job Title	Salary Range
Grade 1	$13,156–$18,644
Shelver	
Grade 2	$15,330–$21,725
Book seller	
Business office cashier	
Physical processing assistant	
Reserves assistant	
Grade 3	$16,359–$23,184
Adult coordinator assistant	
Assistant, business and technology	
Assistant, business office	
Assistant, directory services	
Assistant, outreach services	
Assistant, readers' services	
Interlibrary loan assistant	
Grade 4	$18,075–$25,616
Acquisitions clerk	
Bookmobile driver	
Branch circulation assistant	
Catalog clerk	
Central circulation assistant	
Database assistant	
Delivery driver	
Maintenance technician I	
Media clerk	
Serials control clerk	
Grade 5	$19,906–$28,210
Library assistant	
Library assistant, periodicals	
Mail assistant	
Maintenance technician II	
Personnel assistant	
Reference library assistant	
Secretary	
Grade 6	$19,760–$28,003
Community information database editor	
PC help desk assistant	
PC technician trainee	
Security officer	
Senior circulation assistant	

Job Title	Salary Range
Grade 7	$23,452–$33,235
Business and technology library associate	
Branch library associate	
Catalog associate	
Materials selection associate	
Media library associate	
Outreach services library associate	
Public services library associate (floater)	
Readers' services library associate	
Reference library associate	
Senior security officer	
Grade 8	$26,312–$37,289
Administrative assistant	
African-American resource center coordinator	
Branch circulation supervisor	
Catalog support supervisor	
Cataloger	
Children's specialist	
Communications specialist	
Events coordinator	
Graphic artist	
Interlibrary loan supervisor	
Literacy specialist	
Media specialist	
PC technician	
Personnel specialist	
Purchasing agent	
Grade 9	$29,968–$42,469
Business and technology reference librarian	
Branch reference librarian	
Carpenter	
Catalog librarian	
Children's librarian	
Media librarian	
Periodicals librarian	
Readers' services librarian	
Reference librarian	
Grade 10	$32,318–$45,800
Branch supervising librarian I	
Database supervisor	
Literacy coordinator	
Serials catalog supervisor	
Volunteer coordinator	

Job Title	Salary Range
Grade 11	$35,844–$50,796
Accountant	
Acquisitions supervisor	
Children's librarian (MLS)	
Computer training librarian	
First class stationary engineer	
Genealogy librarian	
Government documents librarian	
Subject specialist librarian	
Web manager	
Grade 12	$33,800–$47,900
Assistant facilities manager	
Branch supervising librarian II/III	
Managing librarian, outreach services	
Supervising librarian, children's services	
Supervisor, central circulation	
Grade 13	$42,636–$60,422
Branch supervising librarian III	
Branch supervising librarian IV	
Managing librarian, business and technology	
Managing librarian, media center	
Managing librarian, readers' services	
Managing librarian, reference	
Supervising librarian, catalog	
Coordinating librarian, young adult and training services	
Grade 14	$46,773–$66,285
Coordinating librarian, adult services	
Coordinating librarian, children's services	
Facilities manager	
Manager, computing operations and technological development	
Manager, microcomputer and networks	
Manager, personnel	
Manager, public relations/trust	
Grade 15	$51,474–$72,947
Manager, automation and technology	
Manager, central library	
Managing librarian, branch services	
Grade 16	$57,585–$81,607
Assistant director	

FIGURE 8.9   Salary Structure for a Small Public Library Using Point Factor and Market Data

Grade and Points	Current Title	Proposed Title	Proposed Salary Range
Grade 1: <500 points	Custodian/delivery clerk Processing assistant III Library assistant I, substitute	Facilities and delivery Technical processor I Substitute I	$14,410–$20,174
Grade 2: 501–650 points	Library technical assistant I Library assistant I Branch assistant I Circulation assistant I	Technical processor I Library assistant I Library assistant I Library assistant I	$15,840–$22,176
Grade 3: 651–825 points	Circulation assistant II Library assistant III, part-time Library associate I, substitute Branch assistant II	Library assistant II Library assistant III Substitute II Library assistant II	$18,343–$26,593

Grade 4:
826–1,075 points
	Processing assistant III
	
	Secretary
	
	Branch library assistant IV
	Library associate I, full-time
	Library associate I, training
	Library associate I, children's
	Library associate I, reference/
	  children's, part-time
	Library associate I, bookmobile
	Branch library associate
	Library assistant IV
		Library associate or
		  technical processor III
		Administrative assistant to
		  the library director
		Library associate I
		Library associate I
		Library associate I
		Library associate I
		Library associate I
		
		Library associate I
		Library associate I
		Circulation supervisor
			$22,110–$32,065

Grade 5: 1,076–1,400 points	Branch library associate II Library associate II, children's Library associate II Library associate II, reference Library associate II, bookmobile Financial secretary	Library associate II Library associate II Library associate II Library associate II Library associate II Finance and facilities manager	$26,538–$39,793
Grade 6: 1,401–1,800 points	Library associate III, special services Library associate III, borrower services	Library associate III Library associate III	$29,150–$43,725
Grade 7: 1,801–2,250 points	Librarian Branch services librarian	Librarian Librarian	$33,787–$50,681
Grade 8: 2,251+ points	Assistant director	Assistant administrator	$45,087–$67,631
Grade 9:	Director		$56,359–$90,174 (Typically contractual and not on salary scale)

the day-to-day running of the library. Figure 8.9 shows not only the positions grouped into grades and the associated salary ranges but also the point factor results for each grade (shown in a range, i.e., 501–650 points for grade 2). This library decided to streamline its titling system while conducting its compensation study, and the example structure shows the proposed new titles as well.

These structures are only *examples*. Again, your structure must reflect *your* library's needs, structure, culture, financial abilities, and goals.

COSTING THE SALARY STRUCTURE

Undoubtedly, there will be a cost to implement your new salary structure because some employees' pay will fall below the minimum of their new grade. Figure 8.10 shows an example spreadsheet for calculating adjustments.

Note that this spreadsheet is for only a portion of the positions you may have. However, it shows the same layout and process you would use for a much larger system. Individual salary data for each employee involved in the study should be included on the spreadsheet. Often, this information will already be in a spreadsheet format available from your payroll or human resources department. You will then enter the proposed grade and minimum salary for each person. If part-time employees are involved, you will need to include hourly salaries as well because adjustments to these salaries will be made on an hourly versus annual basis. This spreadsheet uses a formula to calculate the difference (if any) between the current salary and the proposed minimum of the new salary grade. The total cost impact will be the sum of all of the increases to minimum necessary for your system. We also find

it helpful to calculate the proposed increases as a percent of payroll; this is a figure that boards of directors often like to see.

Although it does not carry a cost implication, you will also need to be prepared to address how you will handle those employees' salaries that may fall above the range maximum. In addition, moving some employees' salaries to the new range minimum may create a compression problem with other employees whose salaries are close to the minimum but who will not receive an adjustment. Based on an employee's experience, performance history, and capabilities, an adjustment to move that person's salary more toward the midpoint (or market rate) may be appropriate. The issues surrounding implementation and salary administration will be discussed in greater detail in the next chapter. The following two sections deal with salaries below and above the range.

Salaries below the Range Minimum

It is quite common that the salaries of some employees will fall below the minimum of the range to which their jobs are assigned. Assuming satisfac-

FIGURE 8.10   Sample Spreadsheet for Calculating Adjustments to Minimum of the Salary Range

Title	Current Salary		Proposed	MINIMUM		Difference to Reach Minimum Range
	Hourly	Annual	Grade	Hourly	Annual	
Administrator	$28.65	$ 52,151	14	$27.25	$49,595	–0–
Information services librarian	20.28	36,913	12	21.00	38,215	$1,302
Automation services department head	28.70	52,227	13	23.64	43,025	–0–
Administrative assistant	19.82	36,077	7	12.73	23,171	–0–
Automation technician	15.67	28,512	8	14.00	25,480	–0–
Automation technician	13.93	25,347	8	14.00	25,480	$133
Library assistant	13.07	23,783	5	10.52	19,151	–0–
Library assistant	12.08	21,988	5	10.52	19,151	–0–
Driver	10.23	15,364	4	9.43	17,154	–0–
Driver	9.83	16,610	4	9.43	17,154	–0–
Total	$308,972					$1,435
Increases as percent of payroll: 0%						

tory performance, each employee's salary should be adjusted to the minimum of the range, immediately if possible or by a phased-in approach if the fiscal impact is severe. A policy of immediately adjusting the salaries of those employees protects the integrity of the new pay system. However, if many employees fall below the minimum, a careful review is required: Not only may the costs of adjustments be high but also equity issues between the employees receiving minimum adjustments and other employees who may be near the range minimum but not eligible for an increase may require further analysis and a phasing-in of compression increases.

If it is not possible to make immediate adjustments to new salary minimums because of the fiscal impact, following are several options you may want to consider:

At the employee's next review date, or when salary increases (cost-of-living adjustments or step adjustments) are awarded, implement the new increases *or* bring the employee's salary to the new minimum of the salary range, whichever is greater.

At the employee's anniversary or review date, add the amount of the minimum adjustment to the planned increase.

The option with the highest fiscal impact, and one not often chosen in academia or the public sector, is to immediately adjust the salaries of all employees to the same relationship to midpoint they had prior to the implementation of the new pay plan. Thus, employees paid at midpoint in the prior pay plan would have their salaries adjusted to the midpoint of the new pay plan. In a step system, the employee at step 2 would be placed at step 2 in the new system.

Salaries above the Range Maximum

When implementing a new pay program, particularly in systems with many long-term employees, it is common to have some salaries that are above the new maximum for the range. In the order of relative cost impact, alternatives to bring the salaries of those employees who are above the maximum into the new range include the following:

Immediately reduce the employee's salary to the new range maximum (not recommended).

Freeze any pay adjustments until future *salary range* increases catch up with the employee's salary.

"Red-circle" or freeze the employee's salary, but grant lump-sum increases at review time or whenever increases are generally granted (preferably based on performance versus simple longevity).

Continue to grant a salary increase, but grant less than the amount of the annual structure adjustment.

Salary compression is also likely to occur during the implementation of a new program. At that time, minimum adjustments are funded immediately, but some employees with salaries close to or at the new minimum do not receive an automatic adjustment. One option to alleviate salary compression is to review each employee's salary and position in the new range, making recommendations for an appropriate equity adjustment, if warranted. Equity adjustments may be made in consideration of performance, education, experience, length of time on the job, relation of pay to the market, and relation of pay to that of others in the same positions. This may be an expensive alternative, but it may be necessary if you are experiencing turnover and equity is an issue.

Another possibility builds on the previous solution—using a phased-in approach to grant salary adjustments due to the implementation of a new structure. Using this method, you would identify the adjustments required and design a plan to bring each identified employee's salary up to the target salary over a predetermined period of time. The time frame should not exceed two years. Other step or merit increases or equity adjustments should not be withheld during this period, or the employee's salary will drop even further behind the market or the salary of other recent hires.

Although it is not wise to ignore these problems, you don't have to recommend and fund compression adjustments. You could raise the salary of employees to the minimum of their new ranges if they fall below without giving other employees an equity adjustment. Employees would then move through the salary range based on performance, across-the-board increases, or step increases. Some public and academic libraries facing fiscal constraints in the implementation of their new pay programs must choose this option, at least for the short term.

9

Implementation

This chapter focuses on the implementation of your new compensation plan. Its two main topics are each critical components of implementation: making salary administration decisions and communicating the plan. These are not linear processes; both are activities in which you will be engaged throughout the life of the project and beyond.

SALARY ADMINISTRATION

Implementation and administration are the next set of decisions needing to be made. This section deals with "what happens next." It covers the salary budgeting process for hiring and moving employees through the salary ranges; step, automatic, and merit pay systems; cost of living adjustments; new-hire salaries; promotions; temporary/acting pay; and policies.

The Salary Budgeting Process

The library's annual budget should include an allocation for salary adjustments for presentation to the board of trustees for approval. This allocation can be segmented into two pools: one for merit increases and the second for other adjustments (such as equity, promotions, within-range adjustment, and so on).

During the fiscal year, the library director or designee (often the human resources director or deputy director) should determine each employee's merit, reclassification, or promotional salary increase. The library director should also annually review and approve recommended changes to the salary ranges as determined through periodic market analysis.

Hiring in and Moving Employees through Their Ranges

All progression methods specify how a person moves from the bottom to the top (minimum to maximum) of the salary range. The major difference among them is the criteria for movement. The major methods are

- automatic increase

- merit increase

- combination of automatic and merit increases

The library does not have to restrict itself to only one method. It may use different methods for different jobs or even different methods for a single job when the employee's salary is at different parts (minimum or maximum) of the range.

Step Pay System (Time-Based)

Many (too many) academic and public libraries divide their entire salary range system into a number of steps. The number of steps is a function of the breadth of the range, the time required to achieve proficiency in the job, whether there are to be steps beyond the market rate, and a determination of the size of a meaningful pay increase.

Step rates facilitate the granting of pay increases by determining the amount of any increase. Of course, it is possible to move a person two steps, but this, more often than not, requires a special approval process.

In a time-based system, time in place or time on the job is the basis for the amount and timing of pay increases. An employee is generally hired at or near the minimum of the salary range. Sometimes the practice is extended to hiring up to step 3.

Generally, step increases are granted annually. However, as the employee moves closer to the range maximum, there may be a two- or three-year wait between step increases, or the step increments may be lower than the "typical" salary increase.

Most libraries with such plans have a structure with many steps (eight to fifteen per salary range). (See figure 9.1.) They usually move employees to the next step once a year at the beginning of the fiscal year or on the employee's anniversary date. In these situations longevity on the job (theoretically) leads to higher proficiency, and the library wants to reward continuity of employment.

A major source of variation in automatic plans is the nature of the maximum rate, i.e., whether it is the market rate or an above-market rate. Libraries that move only to the market rate tend to have salary ranges with a small number of steps and a short time frame for progression. Libraries that move beyond the market rate are specifically rewarding longevity on the job and tend to spread out the progression to the top of the grade over a longer period. This latter variation is common among both public and academic libraries.

Automatic progression does not have to be totally automatic. A fully automatic progression plan is actually a variation of the single-rate or flat-rate system. If all employees can expect to reach the maximum of the rate range after a given period on the job, the assumption is that the maximum is the real rate for the job. Public organizations use automatic progression via steps more than their counterparts in private industry; but this is changing. The emphasis on productivity and flexibility in reinventing products, processes, or services is translating itself into a search for ways to make employees more productive and adaptive. Focusing on performance instead of longevity is part of this trend.

FIGURE 9.1   Sample Steps in a Salary Range

Proposed Grade	Minimum 1	2	3	4	5	6	7	8	9	Maximum 10
4	$11.14	$11.70	$12.26	$12.81	$13.37	$13.93	$14.49	$15.04	$15.60	$16.16
3	10.61	11.14	11.67	12.20	12.73	13.27	13.80	14.33	14.86	15.39
2	9.80	10.29	10.78	11.27	11.76	12.24	12.73	13.22	13.71	14.20
1	8.54	8.92	9.30	9.68	10.06	10.44	10.82	11.20	11.58	11.96

Merit Pay or Pay for Performance

Simply put, pay for performance is a rewards system that links a salary action directly to an employee's performance during the rating period. A pure merit pay system uses an open salary range with only the minimum, maximum, and midpoint defined. Movement within the range is based on performance, and there are no adjustments for cost-of-living or other across-the-board increases. This pay-for-performance system requires an integration of performance appraisal with pay determination. The rationale for merit increases is that the movement to proficiency is actually an improvement in performance and should be treated as such. It should be taken into account that employees differ in their rate of improvement to proficiency, and it is higher performance that the organization wants and should reward.

In all step systems, most employees (good, excellent, or poor performers) eventually get to the top of the pay range. In a merit pay system, the excellent performer should get there faster than the good performer, and the poor performer would generally not receive any salary increases (or not move toward maximum at all). Figure 9.2 shows a pay-for-performance matrix. Figure 9.3 accounts for another variable: This matrix provides for larger (percentage) increases for employees whose salary is in the lower half of their ranges. The percentage of merit pay decreases as employee salaries move past the market rate (midpoint) for the job. One college was adamant that no employee rated less than outstanding would be awarded a salary increase above midpoint. Needless to say, a rule like that requires careful attention when updating salary ranges to ensure that the ranges are, in fact, in line with the market.

Many libraries claim that they use a merit progression system. However, some studies show that as many as 80 percent of employees are at the top of their rate range, belying the use of a true merit system. The problem is compounded when management mixes up automatic increases with merit pay. Granting all employees the same pay increase and announcing it as a merit increase destroys the concept of merit.

Employees should have the opportunity to move toward (or above) the midpoint of their salary ranges or market band based on performance contributions to their immediate work group, their department or branch, and the library as a whole. Pay-for-performance plans move the evaluation mindset from a once a year "event" and entitlement to a continuous process grounded in performance. These plans effectively redistribute the compensation pie available for salary increases in unequal slices.

With a pay-for-performance system, pay becomes a function of two variables:

1. the relationship of existing base pay to market
2. overall performance as measured through the performance evaluation plan

Distinctions in pay through pay-for-performance plans can be more significant than across-the-board adjustments and yet not exceed the merit budget. An example of a pay-for-performance salary matrix that considers both the relationship of salary to the market and performance is shown in figure 9.3. The eligibility for a merit adjustment should be clearly linked to the employee's performance contributions during the review period.

You should be aware of a few potential problems with performance-based pay before making your final decision regarding this type of system. First, many library managers do not have experience managing performance, coaching, and providing feedback to employees. Second, limited salary

---

FIGURE 9.2 Typical Merit Increase

Performance Rating	Exceeds	Outstanding	Commendable	Needs Improvement	Unsatisfactory
Merit increase	6%–8%	5%–7%	4%–6%	2%–3%	0

FIGURE 9.3   Matrix of Salary to Market and to Performance

Evaluation Category	Below Midpoint	At Midpoint	Above Midpoint
1. Results exceeded overall expectations	7.5%	5.0%	4.0%
2. Results fully met basic expectations	5.5%	4.0%	3.0%
3. Results met objectives at a minimal level	3.5%	2.5%	1.5%
4. Performance needs improvement	-0-	-0-	-0-

budgets do not allow for sufficient differentiation of salary increases for employees performing at different levels. For example, if an employee who "meets expectations" is awarded a merit increase of 3 percent and one who "exceeds expectations" is granted an increase to base pay of 4 percent, the extra 1 percent is generally not sufficient to motivate higher performance.

A third drawback is that ratings are often inflated. Very rarely do they approximate a bell-shaped curve of employee performance: More often than not, 80 percent of the employee population is rated "outstanding" or "superior" in a five-category system. Managers do not like to rate someone satisfactory or competent because most, according to employee focus groups, view this rating as equivalent to a "C" or "average" rating, and nobody thinks his or her performance is just average.

Finally, there is a mentality of entitlement in many libraries. It is an unspoken part of the culture. The expectation is that just about everyone will get an increase each year. This expectation is often supported by managers ("makes it easier to manage") and unions ("to ensure fairness and equity") as well, thus making it difficult to change. Unless the performance appraisal system is tied consistently to merit pay increases, either the system comes to be seen as arbitrary or supervisors tend to grant the same increase to all employees, thus destroying the performance-reward connection.

Combination of Automatic and Merit Pay

Some libraries have been introducing merit pay in automatic progression systems that have historically focused on longevity. It is also possible to design progressions that try to balance merit and longevity. These salary progressions usually focus on different criteria at different places in the pay range.

The usual combination in these instances is automatic progression to the midpoint—generally speaking, the market rate for the job—with salary increases beyond the midpoint only on the basis of merit. The rationale for this combination method is that employees can be expected to reach average proficiency within a certain time on the job; this period matches the automatic movement to the midpoint. However, not all employees are expected to exceed average performance on the job, and salary increases above the midpoint should be based on performance that is above average to substantially above average. If your library does a good job of matching time taken to reach the midpoint with time taken to reach proficiency in each job in the salary range, then salary costs are equalized. If these elements are out of balance, then salary costs are higher or lower than is optimum. This combination approach can take one of three forms:

The first possibility has a series of steps from minimum to maximum with the market rate as the middle step. The distinguishing feature of this system can be how movement is determined after the midpoint has been reached.

In a second form there is a series of steps up to the midpoint with an open range from that point on with movement of any percentage possible (within published guidelines) decided by merit.

Another method is to combine longevity and merit at all points in the range. Under this arrangement all employees receive an automatic step increase, but those with above-average performance receive more, such as a two-step jump. In this situation, it is also suggested that you defer increases for those who are not performing well.

Automatic-progression methods of moving through salary ranges are simple to administer since they are purely mechanical adjustments made by time in grade. Introducing merit complicates pay decisions by adding a judgment about how well the person is doing the job and developing a way to incorporate this judgment into a salary increase. This makes administration more complex and, if the judgments are perceived as arbitrary or subjective, raises concerns about the equity of the system. The advantage is that a connection is made between performance and reward, which has been found to be worth the trouble and has served as a transition to a true merit system.

There are some potential negative effects of integrating merit pay in automatic plans if the system was designed to be automatic and variations are seen as exceptions and not the rule. Oftentimes, lack of appropriate funding may not allow for a differentiation of increases based on merit. In many systems that allow for either movement ahead (e.g., an extra step) or denial of increases, these alternatives are rarely used—the problems they pose for administration are not perceived by supervisors to be worth the advantages they offer. For example, one client's performance evaluation tool rated employees using a scale of 1 to 7 for a variety of factors. A summary score of up to 700 points could be awarded. Employees who received a rating of 600 and above would be eligible for an additional increase—if their manager wrote a letter justifying the increase. Needless to say, too many employees received a rating of 590. This system did little to improve morale and is currently being changed.

Cost of Living Adjustments

Generally speaking, it is not a preferable practice to grant across-the-board cost of living adjustments (COLAs), especially in performance-based pay sys-

tems. This practice perpetuates the entitlement mentality of receiving increases without any linkage to the library's goals or to an individual's performance. It is a more effective practice to combine any COLA amounts with the total merit pool and allocate it to employees based on their contribution to the library. However, bear in mind that the elimination of COLAs would be a major change in many library systems and that it is not an easy one to make. If politically feasible, it is a doable and rewarding transition to make.

New Hire Salaries/Recruitment

Hiring a person at or near the range minimum assumes that the library has been hiring people who just meet the minimum requirements and will move them up in the range as they learn the job. However, the new employee who may have years of library or related experience and who can perform all aspects of the job from his or her date of hire with little on-the-job training will need to be hired at or near the market range (plus or minus the range midpoint). Often libraries do not do this, believing that any new hire needs to be placed at or very near the minimum of the salary range, regardless of experience and background. Libraries have lost excellent applicants due to this policy.

In practice, new hires should be eligible to be brought into your library anywhere up to the midpoint of the range. When recruiting for difficult-to-hire jobs, consider allowing a new hire to earn an even higher rate of pay. Starting salaries for new hires should be approved and offered based on

degree of past *relevant* experience

academic credentials or certifications, if required

level of competency to perform the job (at an entry, intermediate, or advanced level)

Care should be taken when considering offering a starting salary above midpoint, since barring a promotion, there is not likely to be ample room for long-term salary growth for the employee.

The salary offer should also take into consideration any pertinent external market conditions that may be hindering your ability to recruit and retain qualified employees in key positions. Often these are not exclusively management jobs, but those that carry out the core business of any organization (without whom the organization would not be able to satisfy customer requests and demands).

Compression

In addition to limiting room for salary growth for the new employee and creating potential budget problems, offering high starting salaries can create another unintentional problem—salary compression—followed by morale issues for incumbents if they learn of the new hire's salary. This is most obvious in the case of new hires brought in at salaries almost the same as or higher than those of employees who have been with a library for a period of time.

Compression can also occur during implementation of a new pay program when minimum adjustments are funded immediately but some employees with salaries close to or at the new minimum do not receive an automatic adjustment. It may also occur when first-line supervisors (such as circulation supervisors or branch managers) of employees in nonexempt jobs (such as circulation assistant or library associate) earn overtime pay that narrows the salary gap. Another instance is when middle management employees are squeezed between top management and the increases given to lower-level employees. All of these examples differ somewhat from the case of new hires in that they involve a hierarchy and the perception of unfairness is related to an inadequate distance between organizational levels.

Solutions to compression depend upon what type it is and how serious it appears to management. There are several ways to respond to it: One obvious solution is to ignore it. This is possible if people are moving rapidly and the problem is mostly one of timing. The person feeling the inequity can be told that it will disappear shortly.

A second possible solution is to adjust the internal structure to reflect external realities. In other words, review each employee's salary and position in the new ranges and make appropriate recommendations for an equity adjustment, if warranted. This may be an expensive but necessary alternative if the organization is experiencing turnover and employee discontent.

Another possibility builds on the previous solution—adopting a phased-in approach to grant salary adjustments due to a new structure implementation or to a direct address of internal compression issues. To implement this solution, identify the total amount of adjustments required and design a plan to bring each identified employee's salary up to the target salary over a predetermined period of time.

Promotions

A promotion is in order when an employee applies for and receives a higher level job (internal promotion) or when an employee's job is substantively changed based on significant and substantial changes in the position's primary duties that have evolved over time (job reevaluation or reclassification). In either case, a promotional increase should be authorized of no less than 5 percent and up to 15 to 20 percent of the employee's pay.

Acting Assignment

An acting assignment is generally authorized when an employee is appointed to a higher level position on a temporary basis, for example, where there is a vacancy that is anticipated to exceed thirty consecutive days. Such appointments may result in a temporary title change and salary adjustment consistent with how other promotions are handled. The amount of the temporary or acting increase, if any, should be based on the following factors:

- level of responsibilities assumed
- assignment of supervisory responsibilities, if applicable
- salary range of the vacant position

The acting pay dollars should not be made a part of the employee's base pay. Rather, a separate check should be issued for the amount of the acting or temporary pay during the approved time period.

Policies

When you make salary administration decisions, they should be written down and become your policies for salary administration. Begin by including your compensation philosophy and job evaluation method. Add sections on job descriptions, salary range adjustments, how salaries are adjusted below the minimum of the range and above the maximum of the range. Include guidelines for reclassifications, promotions, demotions, non–base pay adjustments (incentives) if any, merit pay, and so forth. These salary administration policies should be communicated to employees or, at a minimum, to supervisors.

POSTPROJECT COMMUNICATIONS

The importance of providing ongoing and timely communications to employees throughout the course of the compensation study cannot be overstated. Regardless of the size of your library, it is likely that your new compensation plan will represent a change, perhaps a major change, and a communications plan should be put into place to address it. The goals of your communications plan should include providing

- timely, accurate, consistent information
- information that relieves anxiety
- answers that keep a balance between being overly simplistic and overly technical
- an open, honest place for discussion

Following are some possible components of a communications plan. Review them and see what might be appropriate for your library.

- senior management overview and feedback
- senior management/project manager/review committee/consultant-facilitated overview for supervisor and employees, followed by the opportunity for questions and answers
- discussions of change—why it is necessary and what it means
- newsletters
- brochures
- meetings with staff association/union
- meetings with university/college/county/city human resources personnel and officials
- letter from library director
- frequently asked questions
- bulletins (electronic and written)
- policies and guidelines
- presentations
- small-group meetings
- Web-based tools

To focus your communications plan, you might find it helpful to conduct a force field analysis that will let you know who or what will be the positive and negative forces as you proceed with the implementation of the library's new plan. A force field analysis is used to get a view of all the forces for or against a plan so a decision can be made that takes into account all interests. It helps you plan for or reduce the impact of opposing forces and strengthen or reinforce supporting forces.

Keep in mind that there will be resistance and confusion. Some employees may be unhappy with the outcome of the overall project or process. With the implementation of a compensation program, as with any other program or process involving change, this is normal and to be expected. Your job is to understand that people *will* resist, understand the source of their resistance, and design strategies to minimize it.

10
Trends

This chapter starts with a review of traditional compensation practices used by many libraries and other public organizations and proceeds to a discussion of the challenges that are leading to new compensation and other human resources polices and practices. Strategies for the recruitment and retention of high-performing employees and alternative methods of compensation that are beginning to gain currency in libraries, higher education, and the public sector are also reviewed.

Traditionally, pay practices in academia and the public sector have focused on

cost of living/across-the-board salary adjustments

automatic step increases

longevity pay (salary increases as a reward for years worked
    that may extend beyond the maximum of the range)

reclassifications and promotions as the only mechanisms available
    to provide a "decent" salary increase or incentive for retention

internal equity

classification studies

market-based equity adjustments (too often limited to moving
    employees to the minimum of a new salary range)

This chapter focuses on why some of these common practices are beginning to change as well as indications of future trends.

THE NEED FOR CHANGE

Public and academic libraries are beginning to face the human resources challenges of their private sector neighbors: keen competition for competent, high-performing employees and slashed budgets. The response of some library systems was to reorganize, leaving the roles or jobs of many employees altered, expanded, enriched, and enlarged. Many companies adjusted their compensation philosophies to include pay for performance, incentive versus automatic pay increases, and the elimination of free, costly benefit programs. The concept of "employment for life" was changed to "employment at will." Although aware that change is necessary, library systems, higher education, and many public entities are still finding their way.

In addition to the changes pertaining to funding cuts, five other factors are motivating change. The first is the difficulty of attracting, rewarding, and retaining high-performing employees. More and more of the candidates we would like to hire are taking jobs at the local Wal-Mart or McDonald's, and professional librarians are entering the business world as database managers and systems engineers. Even in a flexible labor market, it is imperative to link compensation to recruitment and retention and create a strategic plan to focus on this issue or the library world will not be able to retain the best and the brightest.

Second, this spectrum of employees is unlike any other and must be recognized and rewarded differently. It is multicultural and multigenerational—retired young seniors are back in the workforce and just as we are beginning to interact with GenXers, we need to learn how to work with, and indeed attract, motivate, and retain, the young members of the Generation Y workforce. We're also seeing retired police officers and members of the armed forces return to work as civilians. Many of them began their careers as eighteen- or twenty-year-olds, and after twenty or twenty-five years of service, are eligible for a full pension and retirement. Too young at forty or so to retire, they are starting a second career. These employees are working side-by-side with mentally and physically challenged colleagues. Libraries are truly reflecting the communities and populations they serve.

Third, we're seeing a greater accountability for productivity. Taxpayers want to know how their tax dollars are being spent, students want to know where their tuition is going, and philanthropists want to know what changes are being made by their donations. Organizational outcomes are studied for almost every new program initiative. City and county council members are asking for strategic plans and productivity measures, and academic VPs want to know how the library is supporting student and faculty learning, research, and retention. Driving this type of productivity is the goal of many new, custom-designed total compensation programs.

Greater risk-taking by many library leaders to plan and implement major change initiatives is the fourth factor driving change. The library leader of today is more motivated to take risks and even ruffle some feathers to productively and effectively run the organization. Many have to—for survival. There is no choice. Change is coming at us so quickly. The library director of a university's health sciences library recently said, "We just dealt with the Internet, now we must learn about portals and PDAs!" Facing each new challenge requires that motivated and competent staff be on board.

Finally, there is the increasing focus on the customer—be it the citizen and taxpayer, sixth grader with a homework assignment, Ph.D. student calling on an archivist for obscure research materials, garden club, freshmen learning online research skills, or customer yelling "You can't revoke my card . . . I returned that book 6 months ago." A focus on customer service is not only particular to libraries; it's increasingly becoming the norm or the other side of the coin to "self-service." Customer service is expected and demanded by the population served by many libraries—even if customers want self-service at times. Library personnel continuously grapple with defining the level of customer service they want to (and can afford to) provide, sometimes striving for the "Nordstrom's model" of very high-quality, attentive, personal service. Providing this level of customer service requires that library staff be highly motivated and competent—often a direct correlation to their compensation.

Increasing the level of service provided to customers resulted in two major organizational design shifts: First, libraries redesigned bureaucratic structures to less-hierarchical, flatter ones with a reduction of management levels. This design change often occurred in conjunction with moving from individualized to team-based problem solving and decision making, the empowerment of individuals and teams to solve problems and make decisions, and a broadening of job scope. All this was supported, at least in part, by the technology that made information available and accessible to all library personnel. With information dispersed and available at even the lowest level, there was no need to centralize power and information at the top. Empowered individuals and teams could easily respond to patrons (now customers) clamoring for service. The second was a shift from a focus on internal equity of positions to one that rewarded performance and paid employees in accordance with the relevant market. The premise of this topic has been talked about throughout this book.

These shifts are actualized in the following, often unarticulated, changing beliefs about compensation shown in Figure 10.1. Review these traditional and new beliefs about pay. Where do your beliefs coincide? What are your expectations of employees? What should the role of middle management be in making pay decisions? How should tenure or longevity affect the pay an employee earns? What role should performance and completion of projects take? By now you probably have a lot of knowledge and some strong ideas about these topics.

FIGURE 10.1   Traditional and Current Compensation Beliefs

Traditional Beliefs	Current Beliefs
We have good relationships with our employees and try to avoid problems.	Every employee is expected to contribute. Our compensation system was designed and is managed as an incentive for employees to use their capabilities to achieve the library's goals.
Compensation is a human resources/county/university function. They manage the program and any salary increases.	Compensation is a management system; human resources/county/university serve as consultants to educate and help managers make pay decisions.
We value consistency in salary management.	Management flexibility is a program goal.
Employees need to know we are paying them fairly, but we do not involve them in redesigning pay programs.	Managers and employees are asked for their input in any pay plan design to ensure that changes are accepted and meet their operational needs.
Pay increases are primarily based on longevity.	Pay increases are primarily based on performance (individual or team) and competence.
We rely on a proven job evaluation system to ensure that pay is equitable.	Pay levels reflect the value and contribution of the employee as dictated by the labor market and individual performance.
Our compensation program is based on internal equity principles.	Our compensation program is aligned with market pay rates.
Our compensation program is consistent with widely used design principles. Many leading employers rely on the same salary management practices.	Our program is based on our needs, values, and the way our organization is managed. It was designed to fit our library.
Almost all of our employees are good people and earn their pay. Salary increases reward them for their continued efforts.	Our managers are expected to identify the best contributors and to make sure their pay reflects those employees' contributions.
Our salary increase budget depends on several factors but primarily on what we can afford.	We rely on variable pay plans to tie rewards to the achievement of our library's goals and to our ability to pay.

Adapted from H. Richer, "Are Public Employers Ready for a New Pay Program?" *Public Personnel Management* 28, 3 (fall 1999): 323–43.

RECRUITMENT AND RETENTION TRENDS

While a detailed discussion of recruitment and retention trends is beyond the scope of this book, what follows are some approaches to better position your library as an "employer of choice" in your community and enhance your ability to attract, motivate, and retain top-flight employees. For the most part, these are nonmonetary strategies that may not cost a cent but will result in change.

Despite the fact that this book is about compensating employees fairly, research indicates that pay is *not* the primary reason why employees leave jobs. Rather, it is due to

- unhappiness with management's not providing enough freedom or support

- current work assignments that are not challenging enough

- lack of growth opportunities—the new job is considered a promotion

- an opportunity too good (financially) to refuse

- ability to earn more money over the lifetime of a career

- quality-of-life issues

It's not all bad news, as there are a variety of innovative methods your library can adopt to retain good employees. A few of those known to be effective include the following:

trained, skilled supervisors and managers Supervisors and managers are held accountable via performance reviews and incentives for keeping good people and are given the tools with which to do so.

flexible benefits packages Most libraries offer little choice in benefits options. They seem to be limited to individual, husband/wife, or family health plan coverage and HMO, preferred provider, or traditional insurance. With retirees in the labor force working alongside twenty-two-year-olds who probably will not work in the library for more than three years, it's time to rethink—and to offer—what the *employee* values. We should bring more alignment to what they *want* and what they *get*. Beyond a basic level of health-care coverage, must all benefits provided be the same? Should the twenty-year veteran employee with forty-six accrued days of vacation earn another twenty this year if she'd rather have sick days that might be counted toward retirement? Or enhanced life insurance? Or an increased contribution to her pension? Or . . .

flexibility in the work environment To enhance your attractiveness as an employer, offer as much flexibility in work scheduling as possible. Library work often allows for part-time jobs, job sharing, and even tele-work for certain positions. With flexibility prized, your candidate pool will increase, sick leave usage will drop, and productivity will increase.

an environment that is both worker and family friendly Most of these types of programs are designed to meet the needs of a changing workforce and to support recruitment and retention efforts. However, many employers experience unanticipated benefits: decreased turnover and absenteeism and increased productivity. Examples of programs that are worker and family friendly include well-baby programs, on-site or close-by day care, backup or emergency day care, baby nursing rooms, financial counseling, employee assistance programs, elder-care and child-care referral programs, wellness programs, digital modem lines in the employee's home, and health club memberships.

opportunities for training and development Employees want to keep their skills and abilities up to date. It is in your best interest to develop the skills you need internally rather than recruiting for the talent. Beyond training, consider providing challenging opportunities for high-potential employees, developing a mentoring program, and structuring opportunities for job enrichment and enlargement. Finally, provide a policy for tuition reimbursement. The value to both the library and the employee in terms of knowledge, skills, productivity, and loyalty should be obvious, yet it is often the first line item to be cut during a budget crunch. It's time to rethink training and education as an investment instead of an expense.

support to employees   This should include support through strong leadership and mentoring programs. Quality supervision and leadership are enhancements to retention, as is providing orientation programs that help employees feel welcome. In addition, be conscious and purposeful in getting employees involved in the library and permitting innovation and creativity on the job.

competitive compensation   Note that increasing compensation is the last item listed. While it is important, money is neither the best nor the only way to support retention efforts.

Each of the methods listed is very broad, and each needs to be reviewed for "fit" and program design to ensure that it is consistent with your culture and needs. While these ideas might also sound like givens, they are far more difficult to implement, let alone support, than you'd imagine, especially in a mature organization that is used to the status quo. Use of these methods, however, is what keeps high performers.

ALTERNATIVE COMPENSATION PLANS

In light of increased financial pressures, organizational redesign, a competitive labor market, an increasingly diverse workforce, and a desire to focus on the top performers in your workforce, it may be time to consider altering your compensation program or perhaps adding options. Compensation strategies are going beyond market equity and internal fairness. Some recent innovations include cash incentives, noncash incentives, skill- and competency-based pay, gain sharing/success sharing, temporary or supplemental pay, broadband-ing, and pay-for-performance plans. Remember that while compensation systems are only a tool, they are a powerful tool to support the behaviors and achievements you want to reward.

Cash Incentives

Incentives are a lump-sum payment or bonus to an employee in recognition of goal achievement. Incentive pay programs help focus employees on the library's goals and objectives by rewarding actual contributions toward reaching predefined objectives. The incentive or bonus is typically a one-time payment not added to base salary. Thus, it is also a fiscally responsible way to reward high performers because the pay raise does not become an annuity. Some believe that incentives are better motivators than pay raises because an employee's pay can be altered (up or down) in different ratings periods, which should happen if pay is to be a motivator of performance.

An incentive program can be designed to include employees at all or a few levels of the library. It can be structured so it is proportionate to the employee's level of responsibility or contribution.

Incentives have become a fairly standard recruitment and retention technique in the private sector. Because of the competitive labor market, incentives are beginning to gain acceptance in the public sector. Incentives can be used effectively in any branch or department to reward individual performance or team or project performance. They can be designed to reward an employee for achieving a project milestone, upon project completion, or as a retention device. One potential downside to these types of programs, however, is that while incentives do make use of pay to focus the energies and efforts of employees on desired outcomes, they may also result in creating inequities in total compensation. In library systems where internal equity is a strong value, this may result in a difficult, albeit not impossible, culture change.

Noncash Incentives

Noncash awards can be given "on the spot" or as a thank you for a job well done. They are not expensive and are easy to customize to employee preference. Examples of noncash and low-cash awards that you might offer include

- project leaders, the library director, or department heads serve up ice cream sundaes when a team pulls together to complete a project on time
- restaurant gift certificates
- library director or board members take employee to lunch
- certificate for manicure/massage/haircut
- free parking/metro pass (for month, quarter, or year—depending on project/impact)
- spot award—$25 to $50 cash or rewards program gift certificate
- training opportunity
- certificate for casual dress day
- "one day work from home" award
- afternoon off award for which the manager does the employee's work and the employee returns to a clean desk and no messages
- award presentation during department meeting/breakfast/luncheon/board meeting/staff day
- variety of small gifts (personalized pens, gourmet coffee sampler, picture frame, gift certificate)
- cookies/donuts/pizza for the department
- movie tickets
- pickup game lunch (Trivial Pursuit, Pictionary, etc.)
- tickets to sporting events
- bowling/shopping party
- pay a student to wash the employee's car
- 15- to 20-minute seated massage in the office for all project employees
- free health club membership (for a month, quarter, year)
- home cleaning or lawn service voucher for one or more visits

Noncash bonuses are excellent motivators: Research indicates that you will receive a three-to-one payback. That is, for each dollar spent on the incentive, the library will receive $3 back in time, energy, or production from the employee. These incentives should be based on what the employee values, not on what you or anyone else might like to have. For example, an opera lover may not appreciate tickets to a rock concert, and a vegetarian is not likely to be motivated by a fancy dinner in a steakhouse.

Skills- or Knowledge-Based Pay

Knowledge- and skills-based pay is a relatively new concept that can be used as an enhancement to a current compensation program or as part of a broadbanded system. This type of system encourages employees to learn as much as they can about their careers by compensating them for learning new skills related to their jobs and the library as a whole. In a skills- or knowledge-based pay plan, the pay of the employee is linked to the number and types of skills the employee is qualified to perform or to the competencies acquired.

Skills-based pay is expensive if used at all levels. It can be cost effective when offset by higher productivity; the need for less staff; and higher quality, more-productive, and more-flexible employees. It can be designed and implemented for all employees, for certain positions, or to reward skill enrichment of incumbents. If you are having difficulty recruiting employees with certain skills, this type of program may also be structured so you can recruit internally for employees who have a high potential to learn but who may not currently have minimum qualifications to enter a technical or difficult-to-recruit position. It can also be helpful for retention because as employees learn more and are able to do more, they are often lured away by libraries and other organizations paying higher salaries. For some positions, the market moves much faster than pay plans that reward employees for length of service and merit.

Gain Sharing/Success Sharing

Gain sharing, also known as success sharing, is any organizationwide or unitwide incentive designed to reward all members for improved performance.

In these plans, "gains," or *measured real dollar savings,* are shared with all employees in the work unit according to a predetermined formula.

Gain-sharing programs focus on improving quality and productivity, increasing the pace of services, reducing costs, and improving employee relations. Employee involvement and information sharing is a critical component of gain sharing.

Temporary or Supplemental Pay

Temporary or supplemental pay is compensation that is in addition to, but not part of, base pay and is designated for a period of time for "hot" skills or special project work. While an excellent concept, its major shortcomings are twofold: First, it is hard to demarcate and justify when the extra project work falls into the employee's regular job versus being "special." This can be a difficult and disagreeable task if the employee and his or her manager disagree. Second, the "add on" to base salary often results in an expensive, permanent pay raise because sometimes management is reluctant to "take away" salary.

Nonetheless, given this current labor market, temporary pay or a separate salary scale is often given or recommended for positions requiring "hot skills." Project pay is rarely as generous as temporary pay for "hot skills." When ranges are wider and realistically reflect the market, when employees are expected to work flexibly and not stay within the four corners of a narrow job description, working on special projects becomes an important part of many jobs. Having said that, if the assignment the employee is asked to undertake is truly of a higher scope and responsibility level, the employee should be given "acting" pay while in that role. As previously mentioned in chapter 9, acting pay should be issued in a separate check that is not attached to the base pay check.

Broadbanding

Created in the early 1980s by two Navy laboratories, broadbanding refers to the combining of existing job classifications and ranges into wider pay bands. While more commonly adopted in the private sector, several public jurisdictions, parts of the federal government, and a few colleges and libraries have designed their salary structures with much broader salary ranges or bands encompassing more diverse jobs with appreciably different pay levels. While broadbanded ranges in the private sector are often 100 percent or more from minimum to maximum, they are usually quite a bit less in the public sector and higher education realms. The ranges are designed this way to encourage lateral transfers instead of promotions, facilitate the ability of employees to enrich and enlarge their jobs without the necessity of a reclassification or promotion, and improve recruitment and retention efforts, especially when competing with the private sector. Broadbanding has also been combined with skills- and knowledge-based pay to provide room for salary growth in a pay range or band for learning the skills required to perform new tasks.

A number of universities, libraries, and colleges have customized modified broadbanded systems: pay plans with fewer grades, wider ranges (allowing for recognition without reclassification or promotion), and the ability to develop people via horizontal movement. In one university, a plan for career progression was made available through broader job descriptions that were designed around key activities or results categorized as basic, intermediate, and advanced. In this instance, flexible policies were written and managers were empowered to make pay decisions to move employees through the range based on equity, competency, market, and budget.

As a tool, broadbanding should be implemented to respond to a need. It can be implemented to encompass your entire structure, to support an organization redesign to a multifunctional team-based structure, to use in combination with skills-based pay, or to respond to challenges in recruiting and retaining employees.

There are a number of drawbacks to broadbanded systems. Most of them revolve around the difficulty inherent in their administration. While jobs are slotted into a "target range" within the broadband, employees often believe that regardless of their position and its duties, tasks, and responsibilities, they will be eligible to earn up to the maximum of the range. Managers also find these systems difficult to administer because they often are not trained to make these types of pay decisions and find it hard to "just say no."

Pay for Performance

While the trend is that some private sector companies are leaving pay for performance in favor of incentive pay plans, many public organizations and institutions of higher education are just beginning to take it seriously. While managers in companies are accustomed to holding the accountability that goes with making pay decisions within open ranges or broadbands, most traditional public sector plans are steeped in the traditions of awarding automatic step and cost-of-living or other increases. Although the option of pay for performance or merit pay was covered in chapter 9, it bears further discussion, as many library systems are heading in this direction because it sends the message that performance is important.

Today, more libraries and other public jurisdictions are moving toward "performance management" by modifying or overhauling their traditional performance evaluation systems. Performance management systems embody the following six key characteristics:

1. Individual performance objectives are tailored to each employee's job.
2. Objectives show appropriate linkage to department or library goals.
3. Interim performance discussions occur between the employee and supervisor.
4. Library-specific competencies are in place that describe the behavioral expectations of all employees.
5. An internal or external customer feedback feature may be included as a feature of the new performance management system.
6. An employee development plan builds on the employee's career and professional interests.

The linkage (from the results of employee contributions through the performance management plan) to pay is clear and more objectively determined than in traditional compensation systems.

SUCCESSFUL IMPLEMENTATION OF A NEW COMPENSATION SYSTEM

Yes, there is hope if your library wants to move toward a performance-based or other new type of system. Following are some keys to the successful implementation of any new compensation system.

1. Make sure you and your management know why you want to make a change. (Many leaders change their rewards system because their buddy's company/library did so.) Make sure you have a clear understanding of what you want the new system to accomplish and why. In addition, remember that you want to reinforce and reward behaviors that support your strategic plan. Therefore, design accordingly.
2. Communicate with employees. You cannot overdo communication. Solicit employees' input and involvement, educate them, and keep them informed as progress is made on plan design.
3. Design a system that is fair, requires the setting of high quality short- and long-term goals, is based on objective measures of performance, can provide accurate ratings, and requires meaningful feedback. Note the term "a system," not a performance appraisal form. The form is only a small part of an ongoing process that should include coaching, mentoring, regular feedback, development plans, and so forth.
4. Train employees and managers in how to use the system.
5. Understand that employees must believe that rewards are truly based on their performance and that favoritism, longevity, or other factors will not rule.
6. Know that moving toward performance-based pay or any new system is a culture change that takes time, energy, and effort. It must be seen as a priority of utmost importance: The library director and senior management must lead it. Human resources, other staff members, and even consultants

can support the effort, but it truly needs to be led by library leadership if it is to be given any life at all.

No longer does the library expect a long-term commitment from employees—such as employment until retirement. Employees work "at will," and often change jobs as soon as a better offer comes along—one that can use their new skills, will offer training opportunities, and will appreciate and reward their high productivity. Employees will have a shorter career life cycle. An implication for compensation in the library is that many will be entering your library with skills and experience that will warrant their being placed above the minimum of the salary range, and they may, ultimately, earn more money than long-service employees in the same position.

Because of these changes—the requirement for increased productivity, a focus on outcome measures, reductions in funding, the need to do more with less and to do it faster/quicker/cheaper—many libraries have begun to rethink their compensation plans. They are doing so in pursuit of tools that will reward the behaviors, skills, and knowledge that the library needs to reward.

Will human resources and library managers reading this book wholeheartedly adopt these new ways of thinking about compensation? No, not yet anyway. Experience with a variety of clients—even public libraries—indicates that many are seeing a need for reward systems that support goals, mandates, emphasis on outcomes and enhanced customer service, technology changes, and a changed workforce. Both academic and public libraries are beginning to make changes and view some of the new beliefs as a helpful way to manage effectively while recruiting, motivating, and retaining top performers.

Although your library may not yet be ready to implement a new pay program, taking steps, no matter how small, toward implementing new compensation programs can be important building blocks for future endeavors on a larger scale. In addition, as employees are made aware of these steps to improve and update compensation programs, morale and motivation can increase. These are benefits too significant to overlook.

Keep an open mind and think of some of these new ways of structuring compensation as possibilities—*if* they fit *your* organization—and as something you might want to plan for in the future.

APPENDIX

Project Work Plan and Time Line

STEP	WEEK
1. Project Planning and Kick-off	
Meet with project manager and others	1
2. Assessment	
Prepare education presentation	1
Meet with compensation review committee	2
Interview library director, department heads, trustees, city/county/university/other officials	1–2
Write and send employee communications letter	1–2
Develop communications plan	1–2
3. Develop compensation philosophy	3–4
4. Classification/Job Analysis	
Draft job analysis questionnaire	1
Issue job analysis questionnaire	2–3
Copy and sort completed job analysis questionnaires	6
Interview employees	8
5. Classification/Job Evaluation	
Develop job evaluation (point factor) system	4
Hold second meeting with employee committee	6
Form subcommittee to evaluate positions	8–9
Develop database and classification report	9
6. Wage Survey of External Market	
Select organizations to survey	1–2
Draft list of benchmark positions	1–2
Develop survey with brief position descriptions	2
Pilot test survey	3
Distribute survey and follow-up	4–7
Market price positions using published data	4–7
Compile and analyze salary data	10–12
Prepare participants' report	13–14
7. Market Competitiveness Analysis	
Develop summary tables showing market position	10
Prepare assessment of broadbanded and other plans	11
Review	12

125

STEP	WEEK
8. Salary Structure Design	
Develop new compensation structure plans	13–14
Assess implementation costs	14
Review with compensation review committee	15
9. Draft Report	
Review with library director and others	17
Review with department heads (individually or as a group)	17
10. Analysis of Base Salaries	
Analyze salary adjustments	18–19
11. Final Report	
Present to library director	20
Present to governing board	21
12. Employee Communications	
Conduct training sessions	to be determined
13. Staff Training	
Provide ongoing education sessions at project completion	to be determined
Develop maintenance procedures	20
14. Develop Administrative Manuals and Maintenance Procedures	to be determined
15. Presentations	
Give other presentations as requested	to be determined
16. Postproject Communication	
Send letter from library director	to be determined
Draft communications plan	18–20

Glossary

Across-the-board increase: Equal pay raises, stated as a flat rate or percentage of salary, given to every eligible (usually satisfactorily performing) employee.

Bonus: Discretionary reward based on individual or team performance.

Broadbanding: Pay strategy that consolidates as many relatively narrow pay grades into fewer broad bands (ranges) with wide salary ranges (typically 50 to 100 percent).

Compensable factors: Attributes selected to provide a basis for comparing job content in a point factor job evaluation system.

Compensation: Cash and noncash provided by the library to an employee for services.

Compensation philosophy: Ensures that a compensation program supports an organization's culture.

Compensation policy: Ensures that a compensation program carries out the compensation strategy while supporting the compensation philosophy.

Compensation strategy: Ensures that a compensation program, consisting of both pay and benefits, supports the library's mission and goals and specifies what programs will be used and how they will be administered.

Competitive pay policy: The strategic decision made by the library regarding which labor markets and organizations to use as comparison groups and how to set pay levels with respect to those groups.

Compression: Pay differentials too small to be considered equitable. The term may apply to differences between the pay of supervisors and subordinates, the pay of experienced and newly hired personnel in the same job, and pay-range midpoints in successive job grades.

Culture: The norms, beliefs, and assumptions adopted by an organization (or that evolve naturally over time in a mature organization) to enable it to adapt to its external environment and to integrate people and units internally. It is strongly influenced by the values of an organization's management team, and it is reflected by actual observed behavioral practices rather than through senior management pronouncements.

Discrimination: Disparate treatment of employees based on factors not related to qualifications, skills, or performance. Under the terms of Title VII of the Civil Rights Act of 1964, the Age Discrimination and Employment Act of 1967 (ADEA), and the Equal Pay Act of 1963 (EPA), discrimination occurs when any compensation decision is made on the basis of a person's age (for those over age 40), race, color, national origin, religion, or sex in a way that cannot be justified on the basis of job-relatedness and business necessity.

Employee benefits: Noncash compensation including income protection, health coverage, retirement savings, vacation, and income supplements for employees provided totally or partially by employer payments.

Exempt: Executives, administrators, and professional library employees, who are exempt from the overtime provisions of the Fair Labor Standards Act (FLSA).

External equity: A measure of the library's pay structure compared with that of the libraries and other organizations in its labor market. As a fairness criterion, external equity implies that the employer pays wages that correspond to external market rates.

Feedback: Information about the state or outcome of a system that can be used to modify or correct a system's operation. As the term is used with respect to compensation, it relates to the process by which information about the status of performance is given to employees by supervisors: Monetary rewards constitute powerful feedback to employees about their performance; nonmonetary feedback (e.g., praise) can provide strong motivation. Performance appraisals are an example of a feedback mechanism.

Flexible benefits: A plan that permits employees to select benefits they want from a menu of choices. Plans commonly include tax-advantaged features and allow employees to select between taxable forms of compensation. Also known as "cafeteria" plans.

Going rate: Wage rate for any job in the library's labor market.

Hourly rate of pay: The rate of pay per hour for a job being performed. An "hourly" worker may be assigned to various rated jobs during any pay period and is paid the "rate" applicable to each job while working on it.

Incentive pay plan: Formula-driven pay plans that are designed to reward the accomplishment of specific results. Awards usually are tied to expected results identified at the beginning of the performance year. The plans can be based on individual or team achievement or project completion. Incentive plans are forward-looking; bonuses are awarded after the fact.

Internal equity: Setting salaries or salary ranges in accordance with each job's relative value to the library.

Job family: A group of jobs with the same nature of work (e.g., librarian) but requiring different levels of skill, effort, or responsibility (e.g., entry-level librarian versus subject specialist).

Job hierarchy: The perceived value of jobs in relationship to each other within an organization. This hierarchy forms the basis for grouping similar jobs together and establishing salary ranges determined by using a point-factor or other system.

Job satisfaction: An indication of how well a person "likes" his or her work, usually determined by a number of factors including pay, promotional opportunities, supervision, coworkers, and the work itself.

Labor market: A place where labor is exchanged for wages. Unique to each library, the labor markets for libraries and other organizations are identified and defined by a combination of geography (i.e., local, regional, national), industry (e.g., libraries), education required and experience, and function or occupation.

Mandated benefits: Noncash compensation elements that employers are required by law to provide to their employees (e.g., Social Security, unemployment, workers' compensation).

Mean: An arithmetic average derived by adding a set of numbers and then dividing the sum by the number of items in the set.

Median: The middle item in a set of hierarchically ordered data points containing an odd number of items or the average of two middle items if there is an even number of data points.

Merit increase: An increase to an employee's base salary based on performance.

Midpoint progression: The percentage difference in wage rates paid between two adjacent grades at the midpoint of the salary range.

Noncash incentives: Incentive payments that are not convertible to cash (e.g., extra vacation time, gift certificates, a reserved parking space, etc.).

Nonexempt employees: Employees subject to the minimum wage and overtime pay provisions of the Fair Labor Standards Act.

Overtime: Under the Fair Labor Standards Act of 1938 (FLSA), nonexempt employees must be paid one-and-a-half times their normal wage rates for all hours worked in excess of 40 in any workweek.

Pay satisfaction: The degree to which an employee perceives little difference in the pay he or she thinks is deserved and the pay actually received. When pay satisfaction is low, the potential for reduced productivity, turnover, grievances, and absenteeism increases.

Rewards system: An organization's choice of cash and noncash motivational elements and the mix of its total compensation program that is used to support its business strategy.

Seniority: Status determined by the length of time an employee has worked for the library, often as the basis for benefits (e.g., vacation) and longevity pay.

Skill-based pay: A person-based compensation system based on the variety of jobs an employee can perform rather than the specific job that the employee may be doing at a particular time. Pay increases generally are associated with the addition or improvement of the skills of the individual employee as opposed to better performance or seniority within the system.

Step pay plan: Standard progression pay rates established within a pay range. Step increases are generally automatic and a function of satisfactory performance and time in grade.

Total compensation: The reward and recognition package for employees, including all forms of money, benefits, perquisites, and services.

Total remuneration: The sum of the financial and non-financial value to the employee of all the elements in the employment package (i.e., salary, incentives, benefits, perquisites, job satisfaction, organizational affiliation, status, etc.) and any other intrinsic or extrinsic rewards of the employment exchange that the employee values.

Index